WOMEN ON DIVORCE

A Bedside Companion

WOMEN
ON

EDITED BY *Penny Kaganoff*

AND *Susan Spano*

DIVORCE

A Bedside Companion

A Harvest Book

Harcourt Brace & Company

San Diego   New York   London

Library of Congress Cataloging-in-Publication Data
Women on divorce: a bedside companion/edited by
Penny Kaganoff & Susan Spano.—1st ed.
p. cm.
ISBN 0-15-100114-6   ISBN 0-15-600462-3 (pbk.)
1. Divorce. I. Kaganoff, Penny. II. Spano, Susan.
HQ814.W64   1995
300.89—dc20   95-20287

Text set in Galliard   Designed by Camilla Filancia
Printed in the United States of America   First Harvest edition 1997   G F E D C B

FOR OUR PARENTS

Claire and Benzion Kaganoff

Lois and John Spano

CONTENTS

Introduction   *xiii*

ANN PATCHETT
           The Sacrament of Divorce   *1*

ANNE ROIPHE
                A Tale of Two Divorces   *14*

PENNY KAGANOFF
           Other Uses for a Wedding Gown   *26*

JANE SHAPIRO
      This Is What You Need for a Happy Life   *39*

CAROL SHIELDS
                  The Marriage Survivors   *60*

ELLEN GILCHRIST
Meditations on Divorce 69

DIANA HUME GEORGE
The Gender Wars 81

MARY MORRIS
Grounds 98

PERRI KLASS
The Divorces of Others 109

ANN HOOD
It's a Wonderful Divorce 119

SUSAN SPANO
An Historical Romance 134

ALIX KATES SHULMAN
A Failed Divorce 153

FRANCINE PROSE
Divorce as a Spectator Sport 166

DAPHNE MERKIN
In the Country of Divorce 178

About the Contributors 191

Special thanks go to our friend Linda Yellin,
the godmother of this anthology; to Lisa Bankoff,
our wonderful agent; and to our editors: Claire Wachtel,
whose vision and enthusiasm gave our project life,
and Ruth Greenstein, whose grace and patience
shepherded us through to the end. We are also grateful
to our many generous friends, colleagues, and relatives
who helped us bring this book about in more ways
than we can enumerate.

INTRODUCTION

$\mathcal{S}$O OFTEN, in casual conversation, women make mention of their divorces to us—whether or not they know that we have been through the dreaded experience ourselves. And when they do, this signals the fact that they've undergone one of life's major changes, increasingly on a par with the other milestones: menarche, marriage, motherhood, menopause, and death.

We are just two of the millions of women who divorce each year. In America today nearly a third of all women who marry between the ages of twenty and forty-four get divorced. What is more, half of all second marriages end in divorce.

Divorce is a radical rupture in a person's life. It leads us to wonder why we marry in the first place, why marriages go wrong, and what it takes in these times to make a marriage endure. Divorce raises issues such as monogamy,

morality, feminism, sexuality, misogyny, loyalty and betrayal, love, self-respect, and self-delusion. It asks us to
question the way we see ourselves as children, siblings,
and parents, and changes the way others perceive us—be
it as failures, pariahs, threats, comrades, or role models.

For Susan, enduring the process of her divorce compelled her to recognize how her romanticism led her into
a disastrous marriage. She had met her husband in college and for the next fifteen years never wavered in her
love for him—or doubted his for her. But then one day
he confessed that he'd been betraying her almost all
along.

It was at this point, when Susan was in the thick of her
divorce, that she met Penny through a mutual friend who
was also a divorcée. Susan was shell-shocked, full of anger
and pain; but more than anything else, she needed to talk
about her divorce with others who had similar experiences. Sharing stories was a source of catharsis and the key
to making sense of the confusion of her breakup.

Penny had more distance on the subject: Her divorce
had occurred several years before and under different circumstances. She had married the proverbial handsome
and successful Jewish professional—and their union was
a misery. Her decision to divorce him was a moment of
triumph, a brave and healthy act. But it caused a rift in
her relationship with her family and the Orthodox Jewish
community that had been at the center of her existence.
Why couldn't she learn to compromise and make her marriage work? they wondered.

Although our marriages ended in different ways, we
were surprised and gratified to realize how many of our

issues aligned. For example, although we both married after the women's movement had galvanized others of our sex, we still put the very concepts of husband and marriage on a pedestal.

As we read the divorce stories we commissioned for this volume, we were repeatedly impressed by how the various pieces aroused memories of our own experiences. Ann Patchett's essay particularly resonated for Penny. In the story of Ann's severance of a Catholic marriage that properly should have ended only in death, Penny found patterns that suggested her own situation: alienation from a beloved heritage, the shame of a failed relationship.

In fact, the more we considered the essays in this book, the more patterns we noticed, never identical, but there nonetheless to fascinate, twist the heart, make us laugh, and complicate prevailing notions about the how and why of divorce.

That marriages often go awry—sometimes even before the vows die on the lips of the bride and groom—comes as no surprise. But for many of the writers in this collection the question is why. "Why do we make these crazy marriages that end in tragedy or divorce?" Ellen Gilchrist asks in "Meditations on Divorce." For her the answer is bound up with the way people often repeat cycles established when they were young—taking wives and husbands who are like their mothers and fathers, failing to understand the "unconscious strivings and yearnings" that compel them to do so. In "A Tale of Two Divorces," Anne Roiphe tells the story of her mother's bad marriage, and then of her own, finally realizing that "I had married a man more like my father than not and that, more like my mother than not, I had become a creature to be pitied. Like moth to flame I was drawn to repeat."

When ill-considered or simply ill-fated marriages fall apart, children are the innocent victims; this truth echoes throughout the essays. "I wish that we could marry a new mate, repair, go on to undo the worst of our mistakes without leaving ugly deep scars across our children's psyches, but we can't," Anne Roiphe writes. "And furthermore the children will never completely forgive us, never understand how our backs were against the wall." Feeling this, Alix Kates Shulman let a bad marriage go on until it finally went sour; in "A Failed Divorce," she suggests that breakups involving children may "take about as long to get over as the age of the children when the breach occurred."

Though not divorced herself, Perri Klass ("The Divorces of Others") watched divorce after divorce strike the families of the children in her son's play group, following them with more than a little titillation—until her son's fears of divorce toppled her from a "lofty peak of secure couplehood." In "Divorce as a Spectator Sport," Francine Prose notes a similar irresistible interest on the part of herself, her friends, and the culture at large for the kinds of big, splashy, celebrity divorces reported by the media— the great public battles of the sexes that incite happy husbands and wives to take sides. And in "The Marriage Survivors," Carol Shields remarks on the fact that— for fiction writers, at least—divorce has tended to seem simply more engrossing than marriage. "Six hundred fast-turning pages without a single marital breakdown; now there is a challenge. Man and woman meet, fall in love, and integrate their unspotted histories. Crises of all sorts arrive, but their marriage holds firm. Really? You expect readers to believe that kind of fairy-tale stuff?"

While onlookers thrill to each new page in messy marital ruptures and scrutinize their own relationships, the divorced live through the process. This is harrowing enough in itself, without the further complications, ironies, and endless delays created by divorce law and lawyers—and the essayists in this collection have a good deal to say about them. In "This Is What You Need for a Happy Life," Jane Shapiro interviews a preeminent New York City divorce lawyer who has never even contemplated getting divorced himself; unfortunately, he finds most of his colleagues a needy and mediocre lot. "And when you marry need with mediocrity," he says, "you get an awful hybrid."

Daphne Merkin confides that she went through two lawyers before she found one she could feel comfortable with—and even that match was far from perfect. "My lawyer is involved in the feminist end of law, which initially alarmed as much as it attracted me: I wanted to make sure she understood that I was not getting my divorce on behalf of the women's movement and was not interested in taking a rhetorical—if right-minded—position that would endanger my chances." Those "chances" had partly to do with child custody, which she notes is being granted with increasing frequency to fathers when the mothers have careers of their own. "In this regard," she writes, "the more vociferous and unyielding claims of the women's movement (which include the devaluation of motherhood and the insistence on a theoretical egalitarianism at home) have done an inadvertent disservice to divorcing professional women who also happen to be passionate mothers."

And in ways beyond this, the advances achieved by the feminist movement have had surprisingly complex effects on divorcing women. In the vanguard of the movement, Alix Kates Shulman drew up a marriage agreement based on complete gender equality ten years into her second marriage; but as the relationship fell apart, she found that the agreement "rested on nothing more substantial than . . . floating goodwill." Our marriages—that is, Penny's and Susan's—came after the major thrust of the women's movement in the 1970s and should have been informed by feminism. But instead, we married the wrong men for the same old wrong reasons.

Diana Hume George ("The Gender Wars") made a different sort of mistake. She chose a feminist man who had adopted "a conscious program of personal growth and transformation"—one of "the good guys." But when their common-law marriage finally broke down, it was, at least in part, says Hume George, because his feminism had provoked his misogyny. "Such men often feel deep if suppressed anger over what they gave up when they relinquished privileges that would otherwise have been theirs. And in some feminist men this rage is directed toward women. If you get in the way of it, you can be in big trouble."

Getting out of a bad marriage seems to some a great escape, managed desperately and just in the nick of time. This is explored by Ann Hood ("It's a Wonderful Divorce"), who married a man she could love as a friend, but couldn't abide as a spouse. Not long after her divorce, she visited a psychic who read her cards and knew right away what she'd been going through. "Funny thing is," he said to her, "you're not at all upset. In fact, you're glad." Jane Shapiro fled a marriage, too, while pregnant with her second child. Years later she finds that she and her ex can't recall ever having had an argument.

Divorce also affords women the chance to imagine what a good—or at least, enduring—marriage would look like, how it would work. For Daphne Merkin, "psychic bartering" makes a marriage run; for Susan, it takes constant adjustments and tinkering. Interestingly, Anne Roiphe and Ellen Gilchrist both contemplate the value of arranged marriages—practical, mutually beneficial unions, in which love might develop only as an afterthought. And for Mary Morris ("Grounds"), another non-divorced writer, the failure of an important relationship in her past has made her understand why she won't divorce her husband, even if the marriage doesn't fulfill all her needs. "Because I'm the kite and he's the string. Because I can't stand the paperwork. Because he'll read this essay and laugh."

Nonetheless, most of the essayists in this collection find that divorce must exist; indeed, that it is as vital as marriage itself. Awful for children and the psyche, never simple or painlessly managed—but a necessary option. As Ann Patchett writes in "The Sacrament of Divorce," "Make marriage harder if you want to. Outlaw those Vegas chapels with the neon wedding bells, require marriage applications modeled after tax forms, but leave divorce alone. It's grueling. I have never known anyone who went into a marriage thinking that they would have to get out, and I have never known anyone who got out simply. To leave, you have to involve the courts. You have to sue the person you live with for your freedom. You have to disconnect your life from another life and face the sea alone. Never easy, blithe. Never."

How hard divorce is! We found this sentiment expressed in almost every one of the essays in this book. From Daphne Merkin who, stranded "in the country of divorce," finds herself without an identity, to Ellen Gilchrist, appalled by the ugly twists of divorce ("How terrible we feel to be walking around thinking dark thoughts about someone we used to *sleep with*"), to Anne Roiphe, who "felt as if the skin had been stripped from my body the first months after my divorce, and I was only twenty-seven years old."

It is our hope that the essays in this book will reverberate for readers, too—whether they have been divorced, are contemplating the deed, or are witnessing the pain of a divorcing loved one. We offer them as consolation, as inspiration, and above all, as fine examples of writing by contemporary women.

NEW YORK CITY
April 1995

WOMEN
ON DIVORCE

A Bedside Companion

THE

SACRAMENT

OF DIVORCE

BY *Ann Patchett*

$\mathcal{I}$CALL HIM my husband half of the time and my ex-husband the other half, but when I think of him it is as my husband. This isn't because in my secret heart I want to be married to him (there is nothing I can think of wanting less), but because I only have one husband and that's him. Like it or not, he has an important place in my personal history. He has a title. I suppose I must be his ex-wife, since somebody told me he married again. It's been six years now. Enough time has passed that I wish him well, in a way that is so distant and abstract it doesn't even matter.

My divorce began less than a week before we were married. We had to drive out to Donelson to the rectory at Holy Rosary, where we had an appointment with the priest who would perform the service. It was a good thirty minutes from Nashville, my hometown, but marriage was a booming business that year and the more convenient priests were already booked solid. We got lost once we got off the interstate and twisted through the dark and identical streets of tract houses with cinder-block foundations. We didn't talk about anything more important than directions. My husband thought I should know where we were, Tennessee being my state, but I hadn't been to Donelson or Holy Rosary since I was ten years old. I also have a notoriously bad sense of direction.

It was June, because that was the month to get married in, and it was buggy and hot. We had been through the weekend of Catholic marriage seminars, nightmare classes full of the nitty gritty of Natural Family Planning (the cool new way to say rhythm) and personality questionnaires ("Which tasks will you do? Which will your husband do? Which will you do together? A. Iron, B. Take out the trash, C. Make decisions about major purchases"). Now we had to see Father Kibby one-on-one, go over a few things. My husband and I were both Catholics. He wanted nothing to do with the Church but was willing to be married by a priest to make his mother happy. For me it was worth more. I was a Catholic shaped by twelve years of Catholic school. Marriage was one of the seven sacraments I had memorized along with my multiplication tables in third grade. Catholicism wasn't at the heart of marriage for me, but it was part of it. Marriage was one of the sacraments I was entitled to.

My hands were sweating from more than the heat when we got to the rectory office. We were late and shouldn't have been. Seeing a priest meant trouble, sin, confession, nothing good, but Father Kibby was young and put us at ease. He wore jeans and a yellow polo shirt.

He even said we should get together sometime for a beer and I was flattered. But that would be another evening. Now it was late and there were a few things we had to get done. He would read from the questionnaire attached to the clipboard and check off the appropriate boxes. The June bugs were thumping against the screen. At the end, he explained, we would sign the form.

Did we believe in God and the Catholic Church?

Yes.

Would we raise our children to be Catholic?

Yes.

Were we entering into marriage lightly?

No.

Was this a marriage that could only be dissolved by death?

Death?

Death. That meant that if the marriage didn't work my only way out was to die. He was asking me to swear to my preference for death over divorce. That was the question and I am no fool so I didn't even have to think about the answer. No, of course not. I would choose not to die. At that moment, before it had even started, I understood how my marriage could end.

I should have understood it anyway, because even going into things I was not happy with my husband. We had lived together for two-and-a-half years before we got married so I had a fairly good idea of how we got along. Not well. It's difficult to talk about divorce without getting into your marriage, and yet I'd just as soon leave my marriage alone. Our general patterns were much like those of any unhappy couple, periods of our screaming and my crying broken up by intolerable stretches of silence. We were not helpful to each other. We were not kind. These are the facts: I married him when I should not have and later on I left. I ran out the door, got a ride to the airport, and bought a one-way ticket back to Tennessee.

People ask me, if you knew it wasn't working, why did you marry him? And all I can say is, I didn't know how not to. I believed I was in too deep before the invitations were ever mailed, before the engagement. Maybe it was inexperience or maybe I was stupid. The relationship had a momentum that was taking us to this place and I couldn't figure out how to stop it until four nights before my wedding when the choice was presented in very simple terms: death — my death — or divorce. I was twenty-four years old. My husband was thirty-one. The only way off a runaway train is to jump off, but at that moment the ground looked to be going by so fast that I was paralyzed. And so I lied. I said yes.

Yes, this is a marriage that can only be dissolved by death.

IT IS RARE, but sometimes I still dream about my husband and the dream goes like this: I am in a big, frothy wedding dress of the sort that I refused to wear when we were actually married. It is shimmering white. My sister, in bridesmaid's seashell pink, is fussing with my hair, my mother is bringing me flowers, the church has the sunny, festive air of the kind of wedding that would resolve a Shakespearean comedy. I am about to marry my husband again, after having divorced him, but I don't know how this has happened. I cannot remember the promise but, surely, I must have promised. I am set to marry him and laced inside this dress, I know I have to stop it, break the world apart all over again. Sometimes there are variations to this dream. I am already married to him, or I am married to him for a third or fourth time and am having to divorce him and there is no explanation. I have no idea how I could have let myself get into this kind of trouble, but here I am.

I divorced my husband not much more than a year after I married him, a fact that I still find myself fluffing up by saying we lived together for four years. But that's a lie, too: it was less than that. Oh, I longed for five years of marriage. I craved ten. I wanted to say, See how I tried? I did everything I could, God knows, there was nothing left for me to do. Sticking it out that one year took every ounce of courage I had. But a year sounds like nothing, not a marriage but a breath, a long date. In my mind, women stopped me on the street and said to me, "Put your one year against my fifteen, twenty, thirty-eight. Put your slim, never-had-a-single-baby hips beside mine, four children. Look at the entrenchment of a lifetime spent together. Who owns this house, that photograph. What you had was nothing."

Of course, no one said this, at least no one who had been divorced. In fact, it was quite the opposite. Without knowing it, I had stumbled into the underground and was given the secret handshake to the world's largest club. The Divorced. We were everywhere. Our insurance man called me the week after I left to tell me my husband had removed me from all the policies and I had to sign in approval because I was, at that point, still married. Our insurance man said to me in a quiet voice, "You don't have to do this. You're going to need to take some time." The receptionist at my divorce lawyer's office called back the next day to see how I was doing. It turned out that the receptionist's marriage had ended too, and this was her first job after having spent half her life as a stay-at-home wife. And when I applied for my own credit card and the woman on the phone said to me, are you married or single, and I didn't know the answer, the woman on the phone dropped the questions and called me Honey. "Honey," she said, "I know."

They had empathy. A word I understood for the first time, because suddenly I had it too. It was, perhaps, my only emotion outside of depression and guilt. Days after I left my husband I propped myself up on my mother's sofa and I watched the guests on *Oprah Winfrey.* I watched women with no education and six children, women without a single safety net beneath them who day after day got their heads bashed into the wall for cold food or misfolded towels or the sheer fun of bashing another human head into a wall. I watched men and women from the studio audience stand up and say, "I have no sympathy for you! Why don't you get out? If someone raised a hand to me even once I'd be out of there. Don't you have any self-respect?"

I leaned forward. I knew that voice. I had been that audience, so long ago I can't even remember it now. I had thought I would never stand for anything short of decency and kindness. I thought that anyone who accepted less must be a willing participant, must like it on some level. But at that moment I wanted to be up there on that stage. I would rise out of my soft bucket chair, unclip my microphone. I would put my arms around the shoulders of the guest and whisper in her ear, "Honey, I know. Things happen that you never thought were possible." I would tell her she was good and bright and brave just for getting out of bed in the morning, because the person downstairs was going to call her an idiot when he was speaking to her at all. I didn't have any children and I had a wonderful family who met me at the airport when I came home and kissed me a hundred times. I had a good education and a lot of friends. My husband didn't hit me, a fact he pointed out often. I was only married for a year and with all I had going for me I barely scraped together the strength to leave. You get so worn down it's hard to think of how you might find a suitcase, much less figure out where you'd go or how you'd get there once it's packed. So when I hold the woman on the *Oprah* show I say, "Don't listen to the audience. They don't understand. When the choice is to die or divorce, it isn't always the clearest choice in the world."

It wasn't just strangers I was starting to understand. My mother divorced my father when I was three. Two years later she remarried. My mother and step-father spent the next twenty years trying to decide whether or not they should stay together. Growing up, I had never faulted her for the divorce, but I hated what I thought was her weakness. My mother didn't want to be wrong a second time. She wanted to believe in all sorts of goodness that didn't exist. She wanted to believe in people's ability to change, and so she went back and back and back, every resolution broken by some long talk they had that made things suddenly clear for a while. I wanted her to make her decision and stick to it. In or out, I ultimately didn't care, just make up your mind. But the mind isn't so easily made up. My mother used to say the more lost you were, the later it got, the more you had invested in not being lost. That's why people who are lost so often keep heading in the same direction.

It took my own divorce to really understand, not just to forgive her, but to think that she was doing the very best that could be done with the circumstances at hand. I understood how we long to believe in goodness, especially in the person we promised to love and honor. It isn't just about them, it is how we want to see ourselves. It says that we are good people, patient and kind.

IF I COULDN'T SEE my way clear to leave my husband before we were married, I hadn't begun to take into account the complications that were ahead. We had a job together, adjoining offices, a split position in an English department. We had an Oldsmobile, a stacked washer-drier. We had his family and mine. We had been married. I had promised, sworn, and I believed I was only as good as my word. But as I slowly began to realize that all the problems between us that I had counted on to change would never change, I started running over the list I kept in my head, a secret tally of things that stood between me and my freedom. The dining room suite? Don't need it. The job? I'll give it up. His parents, who I cared for, who would certainly never speak to me again? Gone. This didn't happen all at once. It was a row of obstacles, each one a little more deadly than the one before. At every turn I thought, not this. I can't give this up too, but then I would. It's remarkable when you stop and think how little you've been getting by on and how much you can do without.

The moment of choice changed everything for me. I did the impossible thing, the thing I was sure would kill us both, and we lived. And I kept on doing the impossible. I moved home and became a waitress at a Friday's, where I received a special pin for being the first person at that particular branch of the restaurant to receive a perfect score on her written waitress exam. I was told I would be shift leader in no time. I was required to wear a funny hat. I served fajitas to people I had gone to high school with and I smiled.

I did not die.

Sometimes I would spend half the morning in the shower because I couldn't remember if I'd already shampooed my hair and so I would wash it again and again, not out of some obsessive need for cleanliness, but because I simply couldn't remember. I would get so lost on the way to work some days that I had to pull the car over to the side of the road and take the map out of the glove compartment. I worked four miles from my house. When I woke up at three A.M., as I did every morning, I never once knew where I was. For several minutes I would lie in bed and wonder while my eyes adjusted to the dark. After a while it didn't frighten me anymore.

In time, a lot of time, after I left Friday's and got a fellowship that allowed me to write my first novel, I came to see that there was something liberating about failure and humiliation. Life as I had known it had been destroyed so completely, so publicly, that in a way I was free, like I imagine anyone who walks away from a crash is free. I didn't have expectations anymore, and no one seemed to expect anything from me. I believed that nothing short of a speeding car could kill me. I knew there was nothing I couldn't give up. Even writing, which was my joy and greatest source of self-definition, I could give up if I had to. Despite what anyone says, no one ever died from not writing. It was a gift. And like any gift that comes in lean times, I appreciated it wildly. I loved it with my whole heart.

I was still ashamed. I was a quitter, a failure. Whatever anyone said about divorce, I owned. One night, years later, clear on the other side of the country, I was giving a boring, obligatory dinner party. Among my guests were a man and a woman, both married but living apart from their spouses because of jobs. They must have been paired together at every social outing, though their missing spouses were all they had in common. Late in the evening the conversation turned to where we had lived in the past. It came out, after a long series of questions, that the woman had been married before, that the husband she had now was her second husband.

When were you married?

"A long time ago." She waved her hand, indicating somewhere back there, dark water. It was a gesture I knew. "Another life."

"I was married," I said. It is a deal I am always making with myself, and always breaking, that I won't tell people this. I don't hide it, but it isn't part of my story anymore.

"Well, there you go," the man said. I couldn't remember why I felt I had to invite him, what social debt I owed him. "Two out of three marriages end in divorce. I'm married, both of you are divorced."

But the woman had remarried. Where did that leave us? "I thought it was one out of two," I said.

And maybe because he was feeling secure with his wife who was a thousand miles away, he shook his head. There can be something cruel about people who have had good fortune. They equate it with personal goodness. "Two out of three," he said.

When you think of the statistic, think of me. I'm the one who did it, I divorced. I pulled the moral fabric of this country apart. Selfish quitter.

Time magazine ran an editorial not long after that, a man crying out for "Super Vows" in this age of disposable marriage. Super Vows would show a higher level of commitment. It would be a more serious ceremony. There would be promises, legal and binding, that the couple would submit to lengthy marriage counseling before divorce, that they could only seek divorce after being married a certain length of time. Divorce, the writer said, had become too easy. Waltz in, waltz out.

Waltz in, maybe. Make marriage harder if you want to. Outlaw those Vegas chapels with the neon wedding bells, require marriage applications modeled after tax forms, but leave divorce alone. It's grueling. I have never known anyone who went into a marriage thinking that they would have to get out, and I have never known anyone who got out simply. To leave, you have to involve the courts. You have to sue the person you live with for your freedom. You have to disconnect your life from another life and face the sea alone. Never easy, blithe. Never.

Nor do I think we should have to wait three months or six or nine, depending on the state, for our divorces to take effect, any more than I think a woman needs twenty-four legally enforced hours between consulting her doctor and having an abortion. Termination is a serious business, but we do not need the state to mandate a waiting period so we can see if we really know our own minds. Three weeks after I left my husband he called to say I had a week to come home or file for divorce. Oddly enough, I hadn't even been thinking about divorce, I wasn't planning any further than five minutes ahead. But since I knew at the end of the week I couldn't go back, I called a lawyer.

It turned out my husband was bluffing, thinking that a tough ultimatum would bring me back. When I told him I had filed for the divorce, he told me he would not give me one. He refused to sign the papers. In the state of Pennsylvania, where we had been living, contested divorces had a three-year waiting period. We would be married for three more years. What choice did I have? I settled myself in for the wait, but it wasn't so long after all. One day the signed papers just showed up. My life in the mailbox, stacked between catalogs and the electric bill. I never knew what brought on his change of heart. I never saw him or spoke to him again. We were divorced.

I JUST RE-READ *The Age of Innocence.* Poor Countess Olenska, so much more alive than everyone in New York. She was better than Newland Archer, whom she couldn't give herself to because she was married. It didn't matter to society that she had been wronged by her husband. They felt her life was over. Thanks to the modern age of divorce, my life was not. I was coming to see that as a blessing and not as something to be ashamed of. I was starting to think that my life was a good thing to have. I do not believe that there were more happy marriages before divorce became socially acceptable, that people tried harder, got through their rough times, and were better off. I believe that more people suffered.

I am still a Catholic, and in the eyes of the Church I

am still married. Perhaps I'm just not Catholic enough to care.

Divorce is in the machine now, like love and birth and death. Its possibility informs us, even when it goes untouched. And if we fail at marriage, we are lucky we don't have to fail with the force of our whole life. Sometimes I dream of an eighth sacrament, the sacrament of divorce. Like communion, it is a slim white wafer on the tongue. Like confession, it is forgiveness. Forgiveness is important not so much for what we've done wrong, but for what we feel we need to be forgiven for. Family, friends, God, whoever loves us, forgives us, takes us in again. They are thrilled by our life, our possibilities, our second chances. They weep with gladness that we did not have to die.

A TALE

OF TWO

DIVORCES

BY *Anne Roiphe*

*E*VERY DIVORCE is a story, and while they can begin to sound the same—sad and cautionary—each one is as unique as a human face. My divorce is the tale of two divorces, one that never was and one that was. The first is the story of my parents' marriage.

My mother was the late fifth child, raised in a large house on Riverside Drive in New York City. Her father, who came to America as a boy from a town outside of Suvałki, Poland, had piled shirts on a pushcart and wandered the streets of the Lower East Side in the 1880s. His pushcart turned into a loft with twenty women sewing shirts for him and before he was twenty-five he owned a small company called Van Heusen Shirts. He was one of the founding members of Beth Israel Hospital and I have a photo of him, shovel in hand, black hat on his head, as the foundation stone is placed in the ground.

My mother grew up, small, plump, nervous, fearful of horses, dogs, cats, cars, water, balls that were hit over nets, tunnels, and bridges. She was expected to marry brilliantly into the world of manufacturers of coats, shoes, gowns, store owners, prosperous bankers whose sons attended the dozens of teas and charity events where she—always afraid her hair was wrong, her conversation dull, her dress wrinkled—tried to obey the instructions of her older sister and sparkle. A girl after all had to sparkle. She was under five feet. She was nearsighted. Without her thick glasses she stumbled, recognized no one, groped the wall for comfort. Her lipstick tended to smear. She chain-smoked. She lost things. She daydreamed. Her father died of a sudden heart attack when she was just thirteen. Her older sisters married millionaires, her brothers inherited the business. She was herself considered an heiress, a dangerous state for a tremulous girl, whose soul was perpetually fogged in uncertainty.

At a Z.B.T. Columbia University fraternity party she met my father. He was the Hungarian-born son of a drug salesman who bet the horses and believed that he had missed his grander destiny. My paternal grandfather was never able to move his family out from the railroad flat under the Third Avenue El. His wife, my grandmother, was a statuesque woman, taller than her husband but overwhelmed by the noise, the turmoil of her American days. She never learned English. She stayed home in her nightgown and slippers, sleeping long hours. My father was in law school. He was tall and handsome with black hair slicked down like Valentino and cold eyes set perfectly in an even face. He was an athlete who had earned his college expenses by working summers as a lifeguard in the

Catskills. His shoes were perfectly polished. His white shirt gleamed. He loathed poverty. He claimed to speak no other language than English though he had arrived in America at age nine. He told my mother he loved her. Despite the warnings of her siblings, she believed him. If she was not his dream girl, she was his American dream. They went on their honeymoon to Europe and purchased fine china and linen at every stop.

MY FATHER became a lawyer for the family shirt company. He was edgy, prone to yell at others; he ground his teeth. He suffered from migraines. He could tolerate nothing out of place, nothing that wasn't spotless. He joined a club where men played squash, steamed in the sauna, and drank at the bar. He stayed long hours at his club. He told his wife she was unbeautiful. She believed him although the pictures of her at the time tell a different story. They show a young woman with soft amused eyes and a long neck, with a shy smile and a brave tilt of the head. My father explained to my mother that he could never admire a short woman, that long legs were the essence of glamour.

My father began to have other ladies. He would meet them under the clock at the Biltmore, at motels in Westchester. He had ice in his heart, but he looked good in his undershirt. He looked good in his monogrammed shirts. He lost his nonfamily clients. They didn't like his temper, his impatience. It didn't matter. He took up golf and was gone all day Saturday and Sunday in the good weather. He made investments in the stock market. He had a genius for bad bets. My mother made up the heavy losses. She had two children and she lived just as she was expected to do, with servants to take care of the details, to wake with the babies, to prepare the food, to mop the floors. She spent her days playing cards and shopping. She went to the hairdresser two, sometimes three times a week. A lady came to the house to wax her legs and do her long red nails. She had ulcers, anxiety attacks, panic attacks. In the evening at about five o'clock she would begin to wait for my father to come home. She could do the crossword puzzle in five minutes. She was a genius at canasta, Oklahoma, bridge, backgammon. She joined a book club. She loved the theater and invested cleverly in Broadway shows. She took lessons in French and flower arranging.

At the dinner table, as the food was being served, my father would comment that he didn't like the way my mother wore the barrette in her hair. She would say bitterly that he never liked anything she wore. He would say that she was stupid. She would say that she was not. Their voices would carry. In the kitchen the maid would clutch the side of the sink until her fingernails were white. My mother would weep. My father would storm out of the house, slamming doors, knocking over lamps. She would shout after him, "You don't love me." He would scream at her, "Who could love you?" She would lie in bed with ice cubes on her swollen eyes, chain-smoking Camel cigarettes. She would call her sister for comfort. Her sister would say, "Don't give him an argument." She would say, "I'll try to do better, I really will."

WHEN I WAS seven years old, she lay in the bathtub soaking and I was sitting on the rim keeping her company. "I could divorce him," she said. "I could do it." Her eyes were puffed. I felt a surge of electricity run through me, adrenaline flowed. "Leave him?" I asked. "Yes," she said. "Should I?" she asked me. "Should I leave him? Would you mind?" I was her friend, her confidante. I did not yet know enough of the world to answer the question. I thought of my home split apart. I thought my father would never see me again. I wondered what I would tell my friends. No one I knew had parents who were divorced. I was afraid. "Who will take care of us?" I asked. My mother let the ashes of her cigarette fall into the tub. "God!" she said. "Help me," she said. But she'd asked the wrong person.

Then she did a brave thing. She went to a psychiatrist. I would wait for her downstairs in the lobby. She would emerge from the elevator after her appointment with her mascara smeared over her checks. "When I'm stronger," she said, "I'll leave him." But the years went on. He said she was demanding. He said, "I spend enough time with you. Go to Florida with your sister. Go to Maine with your brother. Stop asking me to talk to you. I've already said everything I want to say." She said, "I need you to admire me. I need you to say you love me." "I do," he said, but then they had a party and I found him in the coat closet with a lady and lipstick all over his face.

He talked about politics. He read history books. He hit on the chin a man who disagreed with him. He yelled at my mother that she had no right to an opinion on anything. He said, "Women with opinions smell like skunks." She said, "He's so smart. He knows so much." She said, "If I leave him no other man will marry me." She said, "If I leave him I will be alone forever." She said, "I can't leave him."

Week after week, she would say something that irritated him. He would make her cry and then he would scream at her for crying. His screams were howls. If you listened to the sound you would think an animal was trapped and in pain. Dinner after dinner my brother and I would silently try to eat our food as the same old fight began again, built and reached its crescendo.

Finally I was old enough. "Leave him," I said. "I don't know," she said, "maybe." But she couldn't and she wouldn't and the dance between them had turned into a marathon. She quit first. She died at age fifty-two, still married, still thinking, if only I had been taller, different, better. He inherited her money and immediately wed a tall woman, with whom he had been having an affair for many years, whose hands shook when she spoke to him. He called her: "That stupid dame." "That dumb broad," he would say. He went off to his club. He went for long walks. He had migraines.

This was a story of a divorce that should have been.

WHEN I WAS twenty-seven I found myself checking into a fleabag hotel in Juárez. My three-year-old daughter was trying to pull the corncob out of the parrot cage and the parrot was trying to bite her fingers. I was there, my room squeezed between those of the local drunks and prostitutes, to get a divorce. This was a divorce that should have been and was. I had married a man whom I thought was just the opposite of my father. He was a playwright, a philosopher. He was from an old southern family. He talked to me all the time and let me read and type his manuscripts. I worked as a receptionist to support him. Our friends were poets and painters, beatniks and their groupies. I had escaped my mother's home or so I thought. What I didn't notice was that my husband was handsome and thought me plain, that my husband was poor and thought me a meal ticket, that my husband—like my father—was dwarfed of spirit and couldn't imagine another soul beside himself. What I didn't know was that I—like my mother—had no faith, no confidence, no sense that I could fly too. I could even write.

My husband had other women and I thought it was an artist's privilege. My husband said, "If Elizabeth Taylor is a woman, then you must be a hamster." I laughed. My husband went on binges and used up all our money. I thought it was poetic although I was always frightened; bill collectors called. I was always apologizing. We didn't fight so I thought I had achieved matrimonial heaven, a place where of course certain compromises were necessary.

Then after I had a child I thought of love as oxygen and I felt faint. In the middle of the night when I was nursing the baby and my husband was out at the local bar I discovered that loneliness was the name of my condition. I noticed that my husband could not hold his child because he was either too drunk, out of the house, closed into his head, or consumed with nervousness about the applause the outside world was giving or withholding from him. I discovered that I had married a man more like my father than not and that, more like my mother than not, I had become a creature to be pitied. Like moth to flame I was drawn to repeat. My divorce was related to her undivorce, so the generations unfold back to back handing on their burdens—by contamination, memory, experience, identification, one's failure becomes the other's.

The courage it takes to really make things better, to change, is rare and won only at great cost. Yes, we are responsible for ourselves, but nevertheless our family stories course and curse through our veins: our memories are not free.

If my mother had been brave enough to go it alone I might have seen myself differently. I might have been brave enough to let myself be loved the first time around. At least I didn't wait for my entire life to pass before leaping up and away. So this is why I listen with tongue in check to all the terrible tales of what divorce has done to the American family. I know that if my mother had left my father not only her life but mine too might have been set on more solid ground. I know that if I had stayed in my marriage my child would have lived forever in the shadow of my perpetual grief and thought of herself as I had, unworthy of the ordinary moments of affection and connection.

IN TWENTIETH-CENTURY America we place so much emphasis on romance that we barely notice the other essentials of marriage that include economics and child rearing. My mother was undone by the economic equation in her marriage. Money, which we know to be a part of the bitterness of divorce, is in there from the beginning, a thread in the cloak of love, whether we like it or not.

History clunking through our private lives certainly affected my mother's marriage and my bad marriage. Woman's proper role, woman's masochistic stance, immigration, push to rise in social status, the confusion of money damned my mother to a lifetime of tears and almost caught me there too. But history is always present without our always being able to name its nasty work.

The women's movement, which came too late for my mother, sent some women off adventure bound, free of suburb, unwilling to be sole caretakers to find, at the end of their rainbow isolation, disappointment, bitterness. The sexual revolution, which soon after burned like a laser through our towns and sent wives running in circles in search of multiple pleasures, freedom from convention, and distance from the burdens of domesticity, was a balloon that popped long before the arrival of AIDS. We found we were not, after all, in need of the perfect orgasm. We were in need of a body to spoon with in bed, a story we could tell together as well as sexual equality.

But there is more. Divorce is also the terrible knife that rends family asunder, and for the children it can be the tilting, defining moment that marks them ever after, walking wounded, angry, sad souls akimbo, always prone to being lost in a forest of despair. They can be tough, too tough. They can be helpless, too helpless. They can never trust. They can be too trusting. They can accept a stepparent for a while and then revoke their acceptance. They can protest the stepparent for a while and then change their mind, but either way their own parents' divorce hangs over them, threat, reminder, betrayal always possible. My stepdaughter, now a married woman and a mother herself, speaks of her own parents' breakup, which came when she was only seven, as the most terrible moment in her life. As she says this I have only to listen to the tightness in her voice, watch the slight tremble in her hand to know that the divorce seemed to her like an earthquake. The divorce caused a before and after and everything after is tarnished, diminished by what went before.

I wish this were not so. I wish that we could marry a new mate, repair, go on to undo the worst of our mistakes without leaving ugly deep scars across our children's psyches, but we can't. And furthermore the children will never completely forgive us, never understand how our backs were against the wall: They may try to understand our broken vows but they don't. Of course there are other things our children don't forgive us for. If we die, if we withdraw, if we let ourselves drown in misery, addictions, if we fail at work or lose our courage in the face of economic or other adversity, that too will eat at their hearts and spoil their chances for the gold ring on life's carousel. There are, in other words, many ways to damage children, and divorce is only the most effective and perhaps most common of them.

For a while, in the seventies, divorce was everywhere, a panacea for the heart burdened. We were too excited by the prospects of freedom to see the damage that was done. The wounds are very severe for both partners and children. It may be worth it as it would have been for my mother. It may be necessary, but divorce is never nice. I felt as if the skin had been stripped from my body the first months after my divorce, and I was only twenty-seven years old. I felt as if I had to learn anew how to walk in the streets, how to set my face, how to plot a direction, how to love. I had to admit to failure, take back my proud words, let others help me. It was a relief, but it was a disaster. I had lost confidence in my decisions. It took a long while to gain back what I had lost. I understand why my mother did not have the strength to do it, although she should have.

I cannot imagine a world in which divorce would not sometimes occur. Men and women will always fail each other, miss each others' gestures, change in fatally different ways. There are men who cannot love, who abuse their wives or themselves or some substance. There are women who do the same. There are some disasters that wreck a marriage, a sick or damaged child, an economic calamity, a professional failure. There are marriages that are simply asphyxiated by daily life.

But I can imagine a world in which divorce would be rare, in which the madness, meanness, mess of everyday life were absorbed and managed without social cataclysm. It is perhaps our American obsession with the romantic that leads to so much trouble. If we were able to see marriage as largely an economic, child-rearing institution, as a social encounter involving ambition, class, money, we might be better off. Never mind our very up-to-date goals of personal fitness and fulfillment; we are still characters, all of us, in a nineteenth-century novel.

At the moment, now that my children are of marriageable age I have become a believer in the arranged betrothal. Such marriages could not possibly cause more mischief than those that were created by our free will rushing about in heavy traffic with its eyes closed. Perhaps we should consider love as a product of marriage instead of the other way around. Of course those societies that arrange marriages have other tragic stories of bride burning, lifelong miserable submission experienced by women, sexual nightmares, poor young girls and dirty old men.

We are the only animal species that cannot seem to figure out how to pair off and raise children without maiming ourselves in the process.

We can bemoan the social disorder caused by divorce until the moon turns to cream cheese, but we are such fragile souls, so easily cast adrift, wounded, set upon by devils of our own making, that no matter how we twist or turn, no system will protect us from the worst. There is cruelty in divorce. There is cruelty in forced or unfortunate marriage. We will continue to cry at weddings because we know how bittersweet, how fragile is the troth. We will always need legal divorce just as an emergency escape hatch is crucial in every submarine. No sense, however, in denying that after every divorce someone will be running like a cat, tin cans tied to its tail: spooked and slowed down.

OTHER USES FOR A WEDDING GOWN

BY *Penny Kaganoff*

$\mathcal{I}$ WINCE when I recall those bizarrely hand-decorated doors of the dormitory rooms of my alma mater, Stern College for Women of Yeshiva University. When friends express surprise that I graduated from such a parochial, conservative institution, I half-jokingly tell them that I don't regret having gotten married or divorced, but I do regret having gone to Stern. The truth is that the three are inextricably linked, cause and effect, cause and effect. My older sister Leah used to press my buttons by calling the school "Sperm" because even though I was trying my best to be a budding intellectual, Stern was known as the type of place a girl went to get her MRS degree. It was a fantasyland whose administrators scheduled classes on Christmas in the middle of a dead and deserted New York City and thought it perfectly all right to pay us dorm counselors less than our male counterparts at Yeshiva College because, after all, the boys needed pocket money to take out the girls. It was the kind of school that pandered to rabbinic families like mine that felt a little inadequate for living in the Jewish boondocks and worried that their daughters might not otherwise meet the right sort of husbands. (Never mind that I grew up in the thriving Jewish community of Chicago and never even met a gentile socially until I left home—when it came to Jews and Jewishness in America, anywhere outside of New York City was considered diaspora.) So I was shipped off to Stern as a matter of course; Leah escaped her fate and thoroughly sealed mine by moving to Israel.

As Stern custom dictated, when a student became engaged—an event which seemed to take place with alarming frequency during my school years—her roommates would decorate their dorm door in her honor. If the girl's fiancé was a medical student, the roommates might fashion a pair of hearts from a stethoscope and write in calligraphy, "There's a doctor in the house." If you were marrying a lawyer there would be scales of justice or a judge's gavel on your door.

In the school newspaper, alongside my carefully reported articles on Israeli women soldiers or religious cults, was the ever-popular column, Rings 'n Things, that congratulated the newest brides- and bridegrooms-to-be. I and my brainy friends often felt like interlopers on Mars where all this hoopla was concerned. We might have felt alienated, but we couldn't help buying into it. As surely as Abraham and Moses believed that the Jews were the chosen people, we Stern girls believed that we would be chosen by a man who would remake us in his image. I remember seeing roommates working on their door creations for hours, and I seem to recall lots of animated discussions about materials and themes and how to resolve the thorny issue that arose when two (or more) roommates were engaged at the same time. Whose decorations were awarded the door, whose got second billing on a wall in the hallway? A friend recalls that a higher status was conferred on a room whose door was decorated. (It was also rumored that if you slept in an engaged girl's bed you, too, would become so lucky.) Little about the girl or her career aspirations was incorporated into these elaborate door designs, and no one asked if the boys at Yeshiva College decorated *their* roommates' doors.

I wish I could tell you I went to Stern in the 1940s or 1950s, when women didn't know better, when a woman's sole career aspiration was to get married and make babies, and when college was just the best place to snag a better class of husband. But the truth is that I went to Stern in the late seventies, graduated, in fact, in 1980, years after the women's movement had changed the lives of others of my sex. I think of those doors and I am instantly helpless and ashamed to be an unmarried Jewish woman. I'm back in high school and my mother is telling me—her straight-A, honor society child, the last of three daughters in an Orthodox family that prides itself on its unbroken until now, fifteen-generation-long line of rabbis—not to act smart on dates because boys won't like me and I won't get asked out a lot. I'm back in grammar school and my loudmouthed buddy Susie and I have wangled our way into the boys-only Talmud class, and now I've placed first in a citywide Talmud competition. We'll give you the Bible prize (which I've also won), say the less-than-consistent powers that be, but there is no way we will award a Talmud prize to a girl. I want my parents to storm the school, hold my principal hostage, and demand that the prize-givers reverse their heinous decision, their capitulation to religious decorum. Of course, nothing happens. My parents aren't thrilled but don't make a stink. I think they are genuinely puzzled—maybe even a little embarrassed—by their smart, troublemaking girl-child. Ah, how much simpler life would be if only I had been born a boy. I am forced to laugh it off and bury the memory. I wonder how the boy who plucked my prize rationalizes his victory; I like to think he's managing a dubious S&L now, but I know he became a rabbi.

Years later, Zack, my ex-husband, and I are in the process of our no-fault American divorce and have to talk on the phone to discuss some legal detail or another. He tells me he has a new girlfriend and like the well-brought-up woman that I am I make polite small talk and ask him what she's like. It's not the only occasion at which I am involuntarily made privy to Zack's post-marriage social life. She has the figure of a model, he says, knowing I'm battling to drop the pounds I put on when I was married to him. A control freak, he was obsessed with every morsel I ate. I was eating, if only he knew it, to fill the emptiness in my heart.

"And she's bright but not intellectual," Zack gloats. He means, of course, she's not like you, Penny. My mother's warning has come home to taunt me after all.

Some years after that, I bump into Zack's sour sister and she tells me my ex has remarried. *Mazel tov,* it seems that he has found my exact opposite: a Jewish gym teacher.

———

THIS IS the Orthodox Jewish world I came from. For a long time I tried to fit in—above all by marrying the perfect man for a Stern girl, a handsome Jewish lawyer on a partner track in a prestigious firm. But when my marriage became unbearable, and I was losing any sense of myself inch by inch, and I knew I had to leave my husband or disappear completely, I was more worried about telling my parents than I was about telling my husband because here was their pride and joy disappointing them by leaving their son-in-law.

After returning from a depressingly happy wedding of one of my Stern friends, I call my mother and tell her something terrible has happened but I can't discuss it on the phone and I insist she fly out that week from Chicago. When my mother and I meet in Boston and I try to explain the abusive nature of my marriage but I don't go into detail because it's too humiliating, she, who loves me very much, asks me what I did to provoke him.

My parents are devastated by the divorce, so worried for my future that they can't communicate their feelings to me. No one from my immediate family flies in to keep me company for the Jewish divorce, the *get*, which in its archaic ritual proves more debilitating than the antiseptic American version. My sister Leah is visiting my folks from Israel and I ask her to leave the kids with my parents and stay with me, but she tells me, "Mommy and Daddy are in a lot of pain right now and they need me." I'm in pain, too; after all, it's *my* divorce. But I accept what I believe to be a punishment I deserve. An aunt and uncle who live in Brookline, Mass., accompany me to the *get*, their certainty palpable that this will never happen to one of their five happily married children.

My divorce drives a necessary wedge between my parents and me. I learn to live a little more for myself and less for them and what I perceive as their overarching demands of me. I completely stop caring about what the Jewish community makes of me.

OUR MARRIAGE was like a bad Jewish joke: We were a perfect couple; I was always feeling guilty and he blamed me for everything. It was my job to make him happy; Zack did not take responsibility for his life. In his eyes we were glued together. Anything I said or did was a reflection on him.

A few months after our wedding, Zack and I move to Brookline. Near us in our apartment complex lives an old high-school friend of Zack's with his wife and son. Brad is one of the most popular and gregarious members of the synagogue, and Zack wants badly to join his crowd. Brad has us over for lunch our first Shabbat in the neighborhood but refuses our many subsequent offers to reciprocate.

Characteristically Zack blames me, rehashing every detail of our conversation that Shabbat afternoon and finding fault in everything I said or did in Brad's presence. They won't be our friends, Zack concludes, because you offended them in some way. I am the social half of the couple, the one who makes friends easily and with pleasure, but Zack makes me so self-conscious that I begin to doubt myself. I dread having guests over for Shabbat and holidays because as soon as they leave Zack begins to pick apart my actions and words, convincing me that I am crazy and unfit for company. (These wounds have never completely healed. To this day, I remain a strange hybrid:

On the outside I'm very outgoing and comfortable with myself, but inside hides a shy person who worries that she's intruding herself upon another, perhaps making a fool of herself.)

Late one night Brad ties the belt from his bathrobe around his neck and hangs himself from a pipe in his basement, leaving his pregnant wife to discover the body. At the *shiva* she apologizes for having evaded us, explaining that Brad had been severely depressed for months and couldn't respond to our friendship. Brad's suicide and his widow's sad apology slap me awake to the misery of my marriage. There are even times when Zack seems to be trying to choke me to silence me during a fight. I am terrified and unable to catch my breath. I never confide in friends; I can't even tell my shrink about Zack's behavior. Part of this is denial and shame, but I also feel that I owe him a measure of loyalty because I am, after all, his wife. You make your bed and lie in it. A good Stern girl to the end.

I light the Shabbat candles and pray to God to end my unhappiness. I begin to obsess that to get back at me after one of our awful fights Zack, never an original thinker, will copy Brad and hang himself to spite me. I make him promise that he won't do it; if he's in the bathroom for a long time, I pound on the door in panic. Then the worry passes and I fantasize about how wonderful it would be to be a widow, pitied and coddled by a warm and loving community, rid of a mean husband without the disgrace and mess of a divorce. Not long after that I leave him.

ONE DAY, several years after our divorce, I am startled to get a call from my ex-husband. He wants to marry a woman, her name is Miriam, but she won't commit until she has talked to me. I am so caught off guard by the call that I say okay, and I am more than a little curious. By this time, during party chitchat, I have rewritten my marriage into a scenario of hopelessly boring corporate lawyer married to the restless bohemian writer. My conversation with Miriam brings me back to the unpleasant reality that was my marriage and makes me face facts.

She is an Orthodox Jew whose family emigrated from Syria. Her first husband, she tells me, used to beat her and she knows that Zack is a real catch. Her candor amazes me; I thought our conversation would be light and breezy. Apparently this type of premarital investigative phone call isn't all that unusual among Orthodox Jews. My parents later admit that a man whose daughter was dating my ex called them to check him out. My parents, incredibly, said he was very nice, just not for me. "What did you expect us to say? After all, you had married him so we didn't want to say he was so bad," they rationalized. Don't hang out your dirty laundry, so to speak.

But Miriam isn't interested in a casual, insincere reference from me. She frightens me and I feel sorry for her in equal measures. She says more than once that "we girls have to stick together." She asks me if his health was a big problem. Zack has a peptic ulcer, and I tell her I think his condition contributed to his general depression and moodiness. She asks me why we didn't have children. How dare she, I think. But then it sinks in that she must be desperate with fear or she wouldn't be asking. We didn't have children, I think but I don't tell Miriam, because I didn't want them to see how Zack treated me and hate and pity me for it. I'd once heard Zack's father tell his mother to shut up and I understood my mother-in-law better than I had before, but I didn't resent her any less. We didn't have children, I think but I don't tell Miriam, because Zack was always so angry at me that he wouldn't make love to me. I finally tell her that we were very young and didn't want any just then. (I was twenty-four when I got married and twenty-seven when I left Zack; twenty-four may have been ancient according to my Orthodox Jewish family but was a baby to the rest of the world.)

Then she circles in for the kill: Was he ever abusive? The memories rush back of a marriage that was like a war: numbing boredom interspersed with horrific episodes. And so, I admit to her, and to myself, how bad my marriage really was. (Whatever she heard may have scared her off; she never married Zack.) She thanks me politely but impersonally, as if I have just shared my grandmother's sought-after recipe for potato kugel, and promises she will never tell Zack what I have told her.

The next day Zack phones me yelling and demanding to know what I said because Miriam wouldn't share our conversation with him. I ask him what he expected and tell him never to call me again. He never does. I hang up, trembling, remembering how frightened I had been during our marriage of him and his unpredictable, explosive anger. For weeks after Miriam's call I have nightmares that Zack is stalking me and retaliates for my disobedience and disloyalty.

I CAN'T even tell you the exact date when a Massachusetts judge finalized my divorce. It was anticlimactic because the one that really counted, the Jewish ritual *get,* took place months before, precisely three weeks after I decided I didn't want to be married anymore. I had to get a *get*, so to speak, because without one any children I might give birth to in the future would be ostracized from the Jewish community and, according to Jewish law, would only be able to marry other offspring of similarly "adulterous" unions.

A *get* is particularly demeaning for women because the Jewish laws that consecrate marriage and divorce also subjugate women to a passive role in these essential life rituals. Apologists are quick to point out that the law served to protect women in the world of the Ancient East, but at the turn of the twenty-first century I could only see these laws to be a cruel anachronism. As a rabbi's daughter, I had known of several cases in which men virtually blackmailed their wives for a fortune of money or for custody of their children. Zack even told me that a relative had encouraged him to extort some sort of financial compensation for letting me go free. I believe he didn't because he was still in love with me and also a bit stunned by the speed with which I set our Jewish divorce in motion.

The rabbis who preside over the *get* also are surprised and duly uncomfortable about dealing with a woman and an assertive one at that. Because Zack has said that he won't lift a finger to arrange the *get* but will, nice guy that he imagines himself to be, show up if I do all the work, I call the local board of rabbis and plead my case. I am informed that they can't assemble a *beth din*, a small rabbinical court, during the summer and can't I wait until the busy fall season? I castigate them for their insensitivity, tell them my husband is hardly enthusiastic now and may withhold a *get* if we wait. Then basically I steel myself and bulldoze them into importing a *beth din* from outside.

But not before they ask numerous and pointless questions about our sex life and other issues that are not their business. I do the begging myself, without my father or any of my many rabbi relatives as my advocate.

During the proceeding, the head rabbi, who had been a great admirer of my grandfather and knows my father as well, never looks me in the eye, obsessing over the letter of the law—he must ask me at least ten times to verify the spelling of my name—and never offering me a word of consolation. The bill of divorce is handwritten in Aramaic, the document is folded, and I am asked to hold out my hands: I look like a supplicant. Zack is told to drop it in my hands but not to hand it to me—no touching allowed for those passing out of coupledom—and I am instructed to lift the document in the air, and then walk several steps with it stuck awkwardly under my arm, my back to the man who was my husband moments before.

After we leave, the rabbi will take a knife to our *get* and slash it in the criss-cross fashion established by Jewish tradition. In reality, this is a small perforation—somewhat like a ticket being cancelled by a conductor—that prevents another couple with our identical names from passing off our *get* as theirs. But intoxicated by the ritual, I have mythologized even this mundane legal detail, bloated it with significance, and feel cheated that I'm not privy to that deed. I once read a book in which a woman scheduled to have a tumor removed from her breast makes the doctor promise to show it to her before disposing of it. I need the catharsis and finality of this *get*-wounding, and I imagine I am stabbing the *get* until it bleeds like a husband would.

S O O N   A F T E R   my divorce, my mother calls and asks me what I did with my wedding gown. At this time in my life, I have little patience for smugly married, oblivious couples, my parents included, and fantasize that they are all getting divorced. My mother tells me that a young woman in my father's congregation is getting married and why don't we lend her my gown? Over my dead body, I think. I don't want everyone in the synagogue to say as the bride walks down the aisle: There goes poor, divorced Penny Kaganoff's wedding gown. I tell her I gave it to charity, but I really gave it to my friend Karen who says she wants to dye the satin a vivid color and go dancing in it. She never gets around to it, and besides, even if tinted crimson, an old wedding gown would probably still look like a wedding gown. Ultimately Karen and I donate it to needy Russian Jewish immigrants, but when I close my eyes before sleep I see my transformed wedding gown dancing away the nights, and the vision sustains me.

M Y   D I V O R C E   is still recent when a moneyed cousin of mine throws a weekend bar mitzvah on Long Island. I am tired of these affairs, where no one asks what books I've read, only a handful of relatives are interested in how I'm advancing at my job, and everyone quizzes me about my dating life. Indeed, I seem to be the only single person at the hotel who is not in the bar mitzvah boy's class at school. Afterward, I get a ride back to the city with a couple whom I've just met, but that doesn't stop them from asking personal questions. Single people just don't have a lot of rights in the Orthodox Jewish milieu. The bored suburban wife perks up considerably when she learns that

I'm divorced, pries all the particulars out of me, and then pops the big question: "Didn't you feel like a failure when you got divorced?"

And there in that overheated, candy wrapper–strewn Ford, creeping along on a crowded expressway, I have an epiphany, and I cross some threshold through which I'll never be able to return. The bad feelings about myself and my husbandless state, generated by the family gathering, evaporate as I tell her from my heart that my divorce was a brave and healthy act, a moment of triumph that I'll always cherish.

Mrs. Nosy is disappointed, for sure, but I'm still singing when I walk through the door of my apartment.

THIS IS WHAT YOU NEED FOR A HAPPY LIFE

BY *Jane Shapiro*

I WANT TO BE married to one man for life. So far this has eluded me—that's the way I think about it: *so far*. As if, after two marriages and two divorces and many quick, interesting years alone—during which years I've lived exactly as I wanted—it could still happen now. I'll be twenty-one and my sexy, considerate boyfriend and I will marry on a blue day, surrounded by an elaborate, loving, familial community that will ratify and then proceed to sustain our union, and he and I will live productively side by side for six decades, growing daily more tranquil and enmeshed. We'll move to a hot climate and sit in twin lawn chairs and telephone our many grown children. Our gold rings will wear and our fingers will shrink. We'll die married! Still this story seems so real to me.

———

ONE WAY I've been thinking about divorce these days has been in discussion with Raoul Lionel Felder, the famous New York divorce lawyer, whose matrimonial firm is the largest and most successful in the country.

Q: Do people first arrive in your office with great ambivalence about divorcing?

A: Not really. Because by the time they come here, they've been to the priest, the minister, psychiatrist, psychologist, the yenta next door — all these people. So while it's not a Rubicon beyond which they can't step back, the fact is they've usually played out all their hands.

Q: So you don't see people who aren't sure —

A: I see them. I see them. But that's not the profile of the majority of clients, no. Because even the people who say "I just want information" — they don't want information, they want to see if they can get up enough courage, or enough money, and so forth.

Q: Have you often thought "These two people should not get divorced"?

A: What I have seen is two misfits. Where you say "Jesus, they're made for each other in heaven! Why are these people ever getting divorced? Who would want to put up with either one of them?"

FIFTEEN YEARS back in time, Ed's and my divorce is imminent. He phones, from a resort in South Carolina. "It's terrific here!" Ed cries, forgetting he and I are estranged. There are 125 tennis courts. There are lavish plants and lawns. Meanwhile I'm thinking: This guy owes me money. Ed has been my second husband — my real one, as I think of him; every divorced woman has had one real husband. Before the kids get to the phone, Ed has filled me in on the layout of his suite. Two giant bedrooms, a living room, a dining room, and an immaculate, gargantuan terrace now house my lonely future ex-husband as he struggles in South Carolina to get perspective on his confusing, tangled, ongoing life with me.

Divorce, like other traumatic events, causes time traveling—like me, many divorcing people, I imagine, find themselves vividly living in other time places: years ago, or years from now when all this will be over, when what is broken will be fixed. Or you feel like two people at once—an old woman who has lost everyone and a girl whose life is beginning at last.

I'm an ordinary divorcée, vivaciously mourning. I rise in the morning peppy and sanguine; only hours later, a heaviness grows in my chest and I'm near sobbing. I weep for hours, fall asleep still snuffling, then wake in the night with tears running into my ears. The next day, I'm shaky and refreshed; at midnight, I can't sleep because I'm excited, planning my moves.

I call my friends to make crude jokes, talk urgently, overexplain and guffaw; I keep them on the phone too long and call again too soon. Daily, I have ideas! I impulsively introduce myself to new people, make plans to change careers or adopt some children or leave town, write sudden letters to friends from high school, sleep with wrong men: a merry widow, every day.

ED TAKES THE KIDS for the weekend. I can't bear two days without the kids. So I travel to Fire Island to see Benjy, my childhood friend, and his wife and their children—to visit them and their family-ness. On Ben and

Alice's redwood deck, in hazy sun and wet air, I know I've been cast off the planet. How can I be among that vast company, the divorcing or divorced, and be so alone? Morosely, Ben introduces me to three sunburned couples: *"This lady is estranged, poor woman."*

All fall, when not working or cooking, I look at television. A week before our divorce is final, a Tuesday evening finds me intently watching the interviewing of some cover girls. Outside, it's darkening fast. The phone rings and I grab for it—could be my husband. But the line is dead. In pearly voices, the cover girls unanimously maintain that having your image appear in a magazine does not change your life.

I have never understood this construct: does not change your life. If these women are right, then divorce doesn't change your life either. I try saying this to myself, but with a convincing sense that my life is (for the second time, this being my second divorce) about to be over.

People who have gone from poverty and obscurity and struggle and despair to being famous movie actors and best-selling authors will say this too: It doesn't change your life. When patently it does. When anyone can see your life is changed beyond recognition.

THE IMMINENCE of Eddie's and my divorce brings back to me my old tormenting feeling of not belonging to any group, family, or clan. A raucous call from a divorced girlfriend reminds me I'll soon be joining a new family—that of women alone, making bawdy jokes, asserting their exhilaration at controlling their lives, and looking, wherever they want, whenever they choose, for fresh mates.

I want to steal some husbands.

I imagine some married women—my closest friends—dying. Right now they're young, lovely, strong. Suddenly they get painless illnesses and swiftly succumb. Their bereaved husbands and I, linked in shock and grief, begin having dinners together. Helpless, in extremis, each husband and I tell many truths. In a dignified way, we bond. At last, hesitantly, then robustly, he and I have brave, profound, elegiac, joyful sex; tears drop from our four over-informed eyes onto afternoon sheets. *Astonishing, life's bounty. We have found each other.* Except that the identity of the widower changes daily, my fantasy is almost pornographic in its extreme specificity: We take our several children to the Phoenix Garden, and then to the movies on Greenwich Avenue, where we chew jujubes and hold hands in the flickering dark and light. We borrow an eight-room condo at Sugarbush, ski hard and eat chili for lunch; at night the kids sleep curled together like pups.

I actually sit at married couples' tables around town, indefatigable in my frantic loneliness, accepting condolences and advice, and thinking, Do I want him? As if I might slip poisoned powder into my beloved girlfriends' Cabernets.

I see what this is: I don't want to have to begin again and set out and endure trial and error and finally make a husband out of an actual person loose in the world. I want someone who *already is* a husband.

I ASK RAOUL FELDER if he has in mind a profile of the ideal client.

A: No, *I* don't. But generally a divorce lawyer would like a stupid rich woman. A stupid *compliant* rich woman.

It doesn't mean the woman is going to be exploited. It means that there's enough money to get well paid, that the client isn't going to question you, and that the client will follow your advice. It's not pejorative, it doesn't mean you'll do something bad for your client—actually, it's the reverse, you'll do better for her; you'll just do your job and not be bothered. You can't blame a lawyer for wanting those three attributes.

MONTHS PASS and I am still thirty-eight—still young. While waiting for my best friends to die, I start dating.

When you first turn your attention from your husband, your judgment is wild and you can't tell potentially suitable people from entirely wrong ones. As we've learned, there are days almost any man (or woman) in the known world looks like a real possibility.

I find a man. I think he's a possibility. I support this idea with the contention that he and I are culturally similar. Our fathers both went (before the Second World War) to Harvard; the new man and I share a longing and admiration for our dead fathers, those darkly handsome, clever boys bucking the quota up there in foreign Cambridge so long ago. The correspondences between the new man and I are so unlikely as to appear significant: We are grandchildren of Latvian Jews who settled in Newark and sold rags until they got ideas and promptly made, in dental equipment and real estate respectively, two modest fortunes. The new man and I get stoned in his Jacuzzi and I make a fool of myself crying, "*From rags to riches!* I never understood what it meant!"

He's a surgeon and I'm ready for a lover; watching

him cut a bite of steak is pretty much a sexual thing. We love meeting in the hospital lobby and rushing to a restaurant. All summer we sit on banquettes in chilled air, plates of pasta before us, trying to get to know each other, not too fast and not too much. We watch ourselves dialing for reservations, chatting at the theater, moving confidently through a lavish world, availing ourselves, without guilt or regret, of its pleasures—he and I share some romantic dream of being well-heeled grown-ups. This makes us appear to be in love.

The new man is great—competent, energetic, alternately solicitous and remote, well paid. After a couple of months, he suddenly appears distracted and says we are not the lovers I had assumed we had become. He needs to think. He wants time off. You are a passive-aggressive shit, I tell him, and our shared passion vanishes like day breaking.

I sob to a friend about our breakup. She says: "This always happens. This is a typical opening salvo: doesn't hit the target, just starts to define where it is."

My friend Ben, though married, knows many single men. When I beg him, he tries to think up a guy for me, suggesting in quick succession two rich, sentimental drug dealers and a never-married mathematician with a heart condition.

Not long after this, I stopped worrying about remarrying and promptly enjoyed fifteen interesting single years.

Q: I ask Raoul Felder: is there a difference between a man's divorce and a woman's divorce?

A: The dynamics are different if you represent a man.

Q: There's probably more crying with a woman—?

A: More crying. There's more emotionality in a woman's divorce and less punching numbers in a computer. It's much harder when you represent a woman. Because today, in divorce in America, the business is at stake. If you represent a man, you're sitting with a party who has all the records, knows what he's doing, has the business accounts in his control. With a woman, you're outside knocking on the door, trying to get in.

Q: Has a woman ever come in to see you and not cried?

A: Oh, sure. *Sure.*

Q: Who? Women who are just completely fed up and finished?

A: [Looks at me sympathetically] Oh, there are fortune hunters and adventuresses in the world.

JUST THIS YEAR—just this month—I woke early, in darkness, with the fully formed intention to talk to my first husband. Since our parting thirty years ago, I've laid eyes on him three times: twice, we spoke awhile; once, I happened to see him run past in the Boston Marathon (even before I recognized his face, I felt an access of pride: his legs were springy and he was breathing well). My first husband and I had never discussed our divorce, as we had never discussed our marriage—we've never mentioned what we were doing all those years ago. Recently, I gave him a call.

JANE: I have very little recollection of what happened when we got divorced. Do you?

DAVID: Well, I've always had three important recollections. I recall coming home from work one day and the apartment was cleared out: not only you and the baby but also furniture.

JANE: What furniture?

DAVID: Not a lot. We had some furniture. One of your father's trucks came for it.

JANE: I didn't take the furniture!

DAVID: The baby's furniture. And I remember a knock on the door about seven at night, I don't know what month. Two cops were there, and I remember the shine, the light reflecting off their leather jackets. And they handed me something—I think it was a court order.

JANE: It's not in your divorce folder?

DAVID: I couldn't find it. But I deduced that the court order was to pay child support of 125 dollars per— must've been a week.

JANE: Could've been a month. It was 1966.

DAVID: Yeah, it could've—

JANE: Sounds like a month.

DAVID: And I also remember going to New York and not being able to see the kids. Those are the three recollections that have stuck with me over the years.

JANE: Why couldn't you see the kids?

DAVID: One time you weren't there when you were supposed to be. And another time—

JANE: You mean I knew in advance you were coming?

DAVID: Oh yeah. In the folder I found a log, it was interesting, of when I went to see them. Strange pieces of paper, with dates. It says: "January: Jane to Europe. February: Jane asked to delay visitation because of her marriage." And then apparently I saw the kids March

22nd, 1969. And then: "April: Delayed because of death." I have no idea whose death it was—

JANE: My father's.

DAVID: That was your father's death, in sixty-nine?

JANE: Yeah, I got married in February and my father died in April.

DAVID: And then that May: "Not there." You weren't there. I remember knocking and there was no answer. And then in June: "Jane said no because of erratic behavior."

JANE: Whose? [laughing]

DAVID: Well, I don't know! I assume you had determined that my behavior was erratic—

JANE: Oh, this is terrible, this is—

DAVID: And then the visitation stops. I think you were still living then in Washington Square. And the Mexican divorce had been—

JANE: Yes, when was that? When *was* the Mexican divorce?

DAVID: I have a copy of it, so I assume you must have the original.

JANE: I don't have the original of anything.

DAVID: And I've also got all these papers from Ephraim London and all your high-powered—

JANE: He was a civil rights lawyer, I don't know why he—

DAVID: He was your attorney! You had all Park Avenue—

JANE: I know. London had an elegant office. I mainly remember the dresses I wore when I went to see him. I have a sartorial record of that time, nothing else—

it's really embarrassing. But I went to Juárez, I had to fly to El Paso, so—

DAVID: I know that.

JANE: Well, when did—when was that?

DAVID: Hold on. I've got it here—

JANE: [laughing] I'm pretty excited about this—

DAVID: You're "excited." This is just like a reunion then, isn't it?

JANE: This is great!

DAVID: "This is *grreatt.*" Is it?

JANE: No, but it's—it's important, for me anyway, because who's going to be able to tell me about my life?

DAVID: I'll tell you about your life.

DAVID: Yeah, after reading these papers over the weekend, I had so many strange feelings. Okay. How do you want to proceed?

JANE: Well, we *are* proceeding. My memories from that time are so hazy. And one reason I don't remember much, I think, was that I'd been suddenly thrust into another, completely consuming life. Because of course when I left I had one baby and I was pregnant, and then soon I had two babies, and I moved alone to New York, where I got no sleep, I didn't have time to eat, I got up at five in the morning and took care of the babies and I went to school at night. So I was hurled out of the life I had lived with you, you know?

DAVID: Yes.

JANE: Into another life, all alone. I just don't remember a lot from that time. Do you recall anything about our marriage? I mean—how did we *decide* to get married? And who brought it up? And how did—

DAVID: You brought it up.

JANE: I did?

DAVID: You brought it up.

JANE: That's what I figured.

DAVID: One day, I think, you called and said Let's get married. So we did.

JANE: Sounds plausible.

DAVID: Late December.

JANE [gloomily]: I know we had anemone and ranunculus.

DAVID: Do you want the Hebrew date?

JANE: Yeah, I'd love that.

DAVID: The sixth of—either "Teves" or "Jeves."

JANE: Probably a *T*, don't you think?

DAVID: Rabbi Stanley Yedwab.

JANE: Doesn't Yedwab sound like one of those invented words, or like a name backwards?

DAVID: Absolutely.

JANE: "B-A-W-D-E-Y," it is, backwards.

DAVID: Bawdy. We said that at the time.

JANE: Oh! We did? At the time? So that was a memory, what I just said?

DAVID: It was a memory.

JANE: Now, do you remember anything about our marriage?

DAVID: Uhh. I—

JANE: I mean, did we have fights? Probably did.

DAVID: I don't remember fights.

JANE: I don't remember *any*.

DAVID: None. I remember feeling pressure from your father and, less so, from you: "What are you gonna do with your life?"

JANE: But you were in graduate school.

DAVID: No.

JANE: Oh.

DAVID: I was only in school when we first got married, in Ithaca.

JANE: Well, how long did we live in Ithaca?

DAVID: Two semesters. A calendar year.

JANE: I've often wondered. Well, what was our— did we have any relationship, that you recall? I know we did, but do you specifically recall anything about it?

DAVID: I remember a dock we used to walk to. On Cooper River.

JANE: Do you remember having discussions about anything, ever?

DAVID: About me: "What are you going to do that's respectable?"

JANE: That was scapegoating—it seems so now. It was neatly structured. I was sinking and dying. And nobody was saying to *me*, "What're you gonna do?" Also, when I got pregnant, nobody said "Gee, isn't it a little early?" In those days, y'know, it seemed sensible.

DAVID: Well, I don't recall if you were taking birth control pills. I think you were, weren't you?

JANE: Well, obviously at some point I must not've been.

DAVID: It was a conscious choice, therefore, not to continue with birth control. Okay.

———

DAVID: I would have to say I did not know the kind of turmoil you were going through. I had no idea of the psychological pain you felt.

JANE: Did I ever mention anything? I can imagine I didn't. I'm just wondering.

DAVID: I don't think so. But it could've been my insensitivity.

JANE: Oh no no no, I doubt I did mention it, actually. Did I talk much? I think I was silent.

DAVID: You were quiet.

JANE: Did I attack you? I can imagine that too.

DAVID: Attack me? Physically?

JANE: Emotionally. I mean did I get mad?

DAVID: I still don't recall *ever* having an argument.

JANE: Isn't that interesting. I don't either.

DAVID: And that was part of the difficulty I had in understanding why there was a breakup. I suppose retrospectively it seems our marriage was meant to be an escape for you.

JANE: Yes, it was.

DAVID: I was a way out.

JANE: Well, I didn't know what else to do with my life. I didn't *have anything* I could possibly do with my life. And I couldn't work, I couldn't study, I couldn't think. There was this blind pain in my head. For many years. And I guess—it was a desperate thing: "Okay, I'll get married, what else can I do. Because I can't think straight."

DAVID: It's a shame we have to have our conversation by phone. There's so much here, real and imagined. And maybe the prelude to your writing about our marriage and divorce is for us to—

JANE: Well, y'know, I'm not writing about *our* divorce. I'm doing a piece about divorce generally. Which is just one of those things in my professional life. And I could imagine our conversation might end up a paragraph, or a sentence. And I'll interview Raoul Felder, the big divorce lawyer, and that'll be another paragraph. And I'll write some very emotional thing about—maybe what I recall of Juárez (which is almost nothing).

But really, the main thing is, this is about thirty years later. Our lives are moving fast. I thought I'd like to—know what happened.

Q: for Raoul Felder: What qualities make an excellent divorce lawyer?

A: Well, the field attracts a mixed bag. Some of them are good lawyers—very few—and some are just cesspool types. Some are control freaks and some are exploitation people. It attracts the worst. (And sometimes some of the best, but very few.) It's not a complicated area of law. I think it's fair to say of most divorce lawyers that you wouldn't want to have a cup of tea with them. And you wouldn't want to kiss them. There's just nobody home.

Q: So it attracts an unsavory group?

A: "Unsavory" is a strong word. A needy group of people. And when you marry need with mediocrity, you get an awful hybrid.

AS DAVID AND I reminded ourselves, I secured our divorce in Juárez. At once, I forgot it; decades later when I tried to remember, what returned so strongly was an odd constellation of things—heat and pale sunlight and dust blowing, and a grim feeling of timelessness and urgency and sadness, and air-conditioning and the scent of martinis and whiskey sours transpiring from iced glasses. I remember the experience both vaguely and intensely, as if this divorce had been a childhood milestone, which of course it almost was—I was twenty-four.

My younger sister flew down with me to El Paso. (The family, I think, assigned her to do this; it's still astonishing to me that she was there. My sister must've stayed in a motel with me and the next morning ridden with me across the border along with the other charges of our local Mexican lawyer. Down in El Paso, we were this morning's bunch of New Yorkers about to be unhitched fast, in concert, in Spanish. We crossed and recrossed the border in a van, through clouds of dust that hung in Texan, then Mexican, then Texan air.

Later, I think our group drank cocktails in a freezing hotel bar in the middle of the afternoon, me and my sister and the other divorced people. Dark red glow of the bar's interior, relief and camaraderie and pain. The others were older than I and either hectically pleased to be unencumbered or despondent about it or both. In farewell, our lawyer said to my sister, who was twenty-one and engaged to be married: "I'll see you in a couple of years."

I ASK Raoul Felder how many years he has been married.

A: Thirty—I don't know, thirty-one years, something like that.

Q: Could you imagine getting a divorce?

A: I'm not a divorce person myself. I'm not a divorcing kind of person. If people leave me alone, I leave them alone.

Q: But let's say yours and your wife's paths diverged?

A: Things don't bother me, I'm into my own head. I don't get bothered if somebody makes a lousy meal—so you eat out. You don't like the perfume—so you sniff other people's perfume. That's all. It's a simple life.

Q: Right. So why is it that other people are coming in this office, their paths have diverged and they've got to—

A: Because most of the time, I think, people are narrow intellectually; they've put too much investment in marriage. You put a lot of investment in marriage, it doesn't work out. You don't put a lot of investment, you roll with it as it comes.

Q: Like anything else. If your expectation is at the correct level, it's going to work?

A: That's right.

1995

MY LOVER and his former wife still own together, for tax reasons, the house he lives in. When we met, this seemed okay—sensible and modern. But my lover sleeps on the futon they shared, under his wife's childhood counterpane; nearby sits her dressing table, holding makeup and combs and perfume; on his desk is a silver box with bracelets and earrings inside. The bathroom (dual sinks) is a gallery of photographs: They have no children, so over and over, in black-and-white and color, it's just them. She graduates from law school, he catches a fish. Every time you step out of the shower, you meet again the annoyingly fresh-faced couple at their wedding in 1978. One of the pictures is so prized that a duplicate appears in his study, pinned as if casually on the wall. They are splashing in the Caribbean sea! Enjoying honeymoon water play! My lover says: "That picture is not characteristic of us. I don't know who stuck it there. I never look at it." He says about her clothes in the closet: "I don't notice them."

"Well, do you notice when she's sleeping with you?"

This is a tough one. Sometimes she drives the two hours from the city and sleeps in their former bed at his side. It isn't often, but it does happen. They don't make love, or touch at all. (I believe this; they hadn't had wholehearted sex in years anyway; why would he need to invent this, after the amazing stuff he's cheerfully confessed?) They just lie there. Probably he clings to the futon's edge and immediately drops unconscious. Maybe she falls quickly into her own dreamless sleep and wakes wondering where she is. She walked out of this house, for somebody else, five years ago.

Well, it turns out they're not divorced yet—haven't gotten around to it. Almost every day, some of the mail that arrives is addressed to his wife. "Do you notice her mail?" I demand. "Not this again," he says. "No. I don't. It's an occasional piece of *mail*."

And of course she used to cook once in awhile, and his kitchen is still hung with her omelette pans, and her spices are lined up, alphabetized and fading, above the sink. One night while I'm standing under the copper-pot ceiling, the phone rings, and he cries, "Don't answer it!" I answer it. She asks for him: "This is his wife." When, midsentence, she realizes who I am, she hangs up. So is she gone?

He's sick of me. He says *Yes, sue me, I was sad when she left.* He says she left regretfully but irrevocably. He says their interdependence is the merest vestigial convenience, their emotional contact nil. (On alternate days, he says she's his best friend for life.) He says the distance between them is vast and unvarying and immutable and he's so fucking tired of being badgered. He says it means less than nothing that they're not divorced yet; not being divorced yet is fundamentally a clerical oversight; of course they plan to divorce, they can divorce any time.

"How about now?"

"Man, you make trouble, don't you?"

Anybody can see I'm stupid in romance and inclined to believe just about anything. We both want me to think my lover's story adds up. Still, I've learned a simple thing in my complicated travels: If you're not divorced yet, you're married.

DAVID: You gonna interview your second husband too?

JANE [puzzled]: Of course not. I know what happened with him. I talk to him once a week.

RAOUL FELDER tells me: In the beginning when you married somebody you were twenty-five, all you did was pound away; you're two sweaty bodies—that's what the marriage is. And then you realize, "Why'd I marry this one?"

Q: So you meet someone else, or you just decide to leave.

A: And most of the time people end up marrying the same people. A little younger, or sexier, or richer, or this or that. But basically the same people again.

Q: Have clients come back to you repeatedly?

A: Of course! As many as four times—a man I talked to this morning, I've done three divorces for. [Pauses. Reflects.] Give 'em a nice divorce, they keep coming.

Q: That's very interesting—it makes the divorce sound nicer than the wedding.

A: It's more expensive but sometimes nicer. You're giving them freedom. At the wedding, they're selling themselves into bondage. With the divorce, you're giving them happiness, release, a chance to make a better life for themselves. How many times can you say to someone, "Here: This is what you need for a happy life. Go. [glumly] Have a happy life."

DIVORCE has left me high and dry. The other day, after, as I've said, many years of excellent single living, I surprised myself with that thought.

I tell my married friends: "I've changed my mind—I want to live with a man." They all say the same thing: "No you don't."

Whenever I have dinner with another single woman, after a decent interval we say what we want in a husband. We name popular qualities, always the same ones, as if men were truly commodities. Potent, we say. Rich, we say. We all claim to want to mate with independent, mature men, and later in the evening all claim to want younger, gentler, more passionate and malleable ones with beautiful arms and legs.

Everybody always says her cherished fantasy is to be *with* a man but to live in a separate house. Okay, maybe that's impossible. So everybody rushes to say she wants a man who is "very busy." This is a universal wish: busy. I am often the first to assert that I want a busy man—

somebody who has his "own life," who doesn't "cling," who will leave me alone and so on. Who can sit nearby without leaning into the edge of my vision or even glancing my way. Of course we don't want to marry a cold or hard or distant man, but somebody as anomalous, fantastic, as a satyr or unicorn: so independent, so warm. And we'll live with him forever—we'll never divorce.

Rich, we say.

Let him live across town, we say.

We are hard-hearted hannahs. We laugh like maniacs and order more wine.

Nobody says: somebody to care for me alone in the world.

THE
MARRIAGE
SURVIVORS

BY *Carol Shields*

$\mathcal{W}$HEN I WAS a young child back in Illinois my Aunt Marjorie and Uncle Fred came over for supper on Wednesday evenings. My mother made meatloaf on those nights, with lemon pudding for dessert; this was Uncle Fred's favorite meal. Once in a while Aunt Marjorie came alone. After a while she *always* came alone. The ghost of Uncle Fred grew thinner and thinner, though his name oddly persisted. "When's Uncle Fred going to come?" I asked Aunt Marjorie one night. "Hmmmmm," she said, and looked down at her hands, frightened.

Later my mother explained about the divorce. Sometimes married people didn't stay married. You could change your mind; it was allowed. Uncle Fred had turned out to be a "rolling stone." He'd rather be on the road than be married to Aunt Marjorie, who, naturally, was very, very sad about the way things had worked out. She didn't want to be reminded of it; it hurt her feelings. It would be better if I didn't mention Uncle Fred to her again. And I mustn't tell anyone else either; the neighbors, my school friends—they didn't need to know.

This was in 1942. The word *divorce* felt hard, ugly, full of suffering and secrecy. Some people at that time associated divorce with movie stars, with glamour, but I didn't. My aunt, a woman in her late thirties, went to night school to learn typing and shorthand, and later found an office job with Magnavox. She lived alone in a small Cleveland apartment; she sent her nieces and nephews birthday cards with dollar bills enclosed; she grew old, developed severe osteoporosis, moved to a Florida trailer park, and died in her bathtub. In all those years the only contact she had with Uncle Fred was a valentine he mailed from California—no return address—in the midfifties. The thought of this whimsical greeting fills me with horror: Uncle Fred's careless act of sentimentality rattling down on my aunt's smashed heart. She bore that as she had borne her other injuries, and the divorce—*her* divorce—seemed almost to disfigure her with time, its molecules joined to her fragile bone structure, her powdery skin, her humility, her lack of ease in the world.

Divorce in those days was rare, and its scattered victims were stamped with failure. Today's higher divorce rate dilutes blame, some believe, invoking the old raspberry jam analogy: the farther you spread it the thinner it gets. It's no one's fault. The stresses of contemporary life are cited. People's expectations are too high. Or too low. There's too much intervention or not enough. Power struggle. Communication problems. Cost of living. Sexual dysfunction. Co-dependence. Inability to establish intimacy.

Victim, victimizer. A subtle inversion has taken place in our thinking, and we remark what a wonder it is, really, considering all the pungently labeled enemies of conjugality, that marriages sometimes survive.

And yet they do. Despite the fact that the divorce rate in North America stands near the 50 percent mark, almost all the people I know are married. Not only married, but involved in long, established, ongoing marriages, thirty years, forty years. Is it by accident that theirs are the faces I find most often around our dining-room table, conversing, reminiscing, toasting each other's anniversaries, and giving an altogether convincing performance of people who are at ease with one another? And news comes from the wider world, too, as year after year Christmas greetings arrive from Tom and Marvie in Toronto, Judy and Sam in London, Dot and Al in California. Our married friends. Still together. Still breathing the old trusted oxygen of matrimony.

I understand the textures of these particular seasoned marriages; after all, they're very like my own. I apprehend the compromises, the unspoken bargains, the rituals, and the jokes, too — the biggest joke being that a good many of us are astonished to find ourselves citizens of the undivorced world, part of a robust kicking chorus, the fortunate few who have fallen through a rent in today's statistical charts. We've had a lucky escape — and we know it — from the tug of social evolution and can't help feeling that there's something just a little bit ludicrous about our situation.

There's something worrying about this, too, for what is it that draws us toward those whose domestic arrangements mirror our own? Surely we don't consciously, or unconsciously either, reject the company of the single and the divorced. What could be more unpardonably smug? And yet, there does seem, when I sit down to review my various tiers of friendship, a preponderance of those like ourselves, the marriage survivors, our comrades in a baffling demographic warp. Why?

Might our flocking together suggest egregious self-congratulations? Did we "try harder"? Did we unwind with greater care the skeins of consequence or were we simply fortunate enough to marry at a time when there were fewer guarantees for parts and services? Are we less sexually imaginative? Or too complacent to countenance disruption—putting the house on the market, breaking the news to the children? Is it a question of temperament that draws us together, a willingness to shrug and put up with things while *they* had the courage to cry halt?

Or is it the thought of the emotional gulf that divides us from the divorced? The divorced and separated know, as we can't possibly know, that dark zone that surrounds the cessation of love. We've never had our life cleft by a moment of decision, that particular morning—I always imagine *it* happening on a Monday morning in November, wind, sleet, the window rattling in its frame—when it is understood, finally, that the shared life, that which has been pledged, sealed, and witnessed, is about to be withdrawn.

IF THERE EXISTS a negative statistical deformation among my own circle of friends, there is an inverse bulge in the world of fiction. Here the divorce curve runs wildly out of range. In literary novels, in works of popular romance, in mysteries, in science fiction, from genre to genre and sparing none—the line on the graph climbs straight up, leaving America's 50 percent divorce figures in the shadows of an impossibly innocent time.

Ask yourself when you last read a novel about a happily married couple. For one reason or another, enduring marriages find little space on the printed page. How is a novelist to pump the necessary tension into the lives of the happily committed? Even the suggestion of a sound marital relationship posits the suspicion of what is being hidden and about to be revealed in a forthcoming chapter. Couples who have good sex, who discuss and resolve their differences, and who care deeply about their bonds of loyalty are clearly as simpleminded and unimaginative as their creator. There they sit with their hobbies and their wallpaper and their cups of decaffeinated coffee, finishing each other's sentences and nodding agreement. She sends his winter coat to the cleaners and frets about his asthma. He continues to find her aging body erotic and he's also extremely fond of her way with grilled peppers. This is all very well, but what can be *done* with folks so narratively unpromising?

It might be thought that novelists would come running forward to pick up the gauntlet. Six hundred fast-turning pages without a single marital breakdown; now there is a challenge. Man and woman meet, fall in love, and integrate their unspotted histories. Crises of all sorts arrive, but their marriage holds firm. Really? You expect readers to believe that kind of fairy-tale stuff?

As a marriage survivor—thirty-eight years—I would like to write that book. I've tried to write it. The modern novel may not be a glass reflecting life back to us, but shouldn't we at least be able to find a measure of congruity between what we experience and what we imagine? We depend on contemporary literature to bring us bulletins from the frontier, just as we look to the literature of previous centuries for an outline of societal patterns. Why then do today's novelists distort the state of marriage by concentrating on connubial disarray? To this I can only cry *mea culpa*, for, despite my long, happy marriage, my novels and short stories are as filled with divorce as any other writer's.

An early novel, *Happenstance* (1980), is as close as I've come to presenting a picture of married contentment. In this book Jack and Brenda Bowman have been married for twenty years. They speak to each other kindly, they honor their vows of fidelity, and they still have fulfilling sex; it's right there in Chapter 3. A number of their friends, though, have gone through divorce, and this casts a shadow over their own happiness. Brenda wonders how the divorced cope with the detritus of all those married years. Like all couples, she and Jack have built up a hoard of shared anecdotes, their private stock, exquisitely flavored by the retelling. The timing and phrasing of these accounts have reached a state of near perfection. Brenda wonders what happens to such stories when couples separate; do they cease to exist? How do people bear such a loss?

As the novel opens both Brenda and Jack are experiencing undefined feelings of restlessness, and, during a week spent apart, they toy with images of temptation. The two of them are as close as people can be after twenty years, and yet they remain, ultimately, strangers, one to the other. The distance between them is wide as a football field; it is also delicately gauged. Anything could knock

by

CAROL
SHIELDS

them off course. This novel about a happy marriage, then, is fueled by the fear of its loss and the possibility of a diminished life.

Tom Avery, the hero of my 1992 novel, *The Republic of Love*, has been divorced not once, but three times. His marriages lie strewn about him. Quickies. He tells himself he's been unlucky, but only half believes it. He lives in a small city where at any moment he's likely to run into his ex-wives or one of his six ex-parents-in-law. There isn't a day when he doesn't feel his three failed marriages pressing down on him. He hates the thought of meeting his old drinking mates who like to kid him about rice coming out of his ears, about going for the *Guinness Book of Records,* about buying the Wedding March on compact disk. Friday nights are spent, dismally, in a community center with the members of the Newly Singles Club, companion divorcées who long to repair their lives and perhaps meet someone new. The program rotates every six months, and by now Tom has heard a variety of lectures on such subjects as "The Ghettoization of the Single in Contemporary Urban Society," which introduces three key coping strategies: bonding, rebonding and disbonding. He is beginning to weary of these talks, and has grown skeptical of the way in which human behavior divides itself into categories of three. Nevertheless, at forty years old he's out looking, once again, perhaps foolishly, for the kind of married love that lasts.

Luckily he has a few married friends, but he's noticed that he's seldom included anymore in their dinner parties. Instead he's more likely to be asked for brunch, joining the family around the table for waffles, or to participate, perhaps, in a backyard project. He feels obliged now to earn his invitations with gifts of fresh flowers or bottles of expensive wine. He admires his friends' babies and dutifully bounces them on his knee in hearty faux-uncle fashion. In return, these married friends dispense well-meaning advice, and occasionally fix him up with single women. Blind dates, though, have become a nightmare, since they lead straight to the agonizing moment when he must confess the details of his splattered history and brace himself for the inevitable response. "Three! You were married three times!" The novel is a love story, employing the classic pattern of enchantment, rupture, and reconciliation, but in the end it is driven less by love than by the failure of love.

Another early novel, *The Box Garden* (1977), should have been a warning to me of the danger of writing about unlived experience. Charleen and Watson, the divorced couple in the book, meet by accident after twelve years of separation, but the encounter felt flat on the page, so flat, in fact, that my two editors, both divorced themselves, asked me if I would rethink the scene. They urged me to show greater "intensity" and "strangeness," and the "bittersweet resonance" such a meeting would arouse. I took their advice, setting the scene up more carefully and turning the emotional thermostat to high. But today, re-reading the section, I find Charleen's reaction forced.

> A twisting breathlessness like a rising funnel-shaped cloud of anguish pressed on my lungs, robbing me of speech and, for a moment, of coherence.

Oh, my. More like a purple-shaped cloud of incomprehension!

STILL, THE FACT IS I *would* like to see more marital equity in the pages of our fiction. And I'd be willing to honor the principle of mimesis and settle for a straight 50 percent success/failure rate. Coupledom, especially when seen in an unsparing light, should not necessarily equal boredom, should it? It might be interesting to see novelists look inside their own specific human packaging and admit that a long marriage—the union of two souls, the merging of contraries, whatever—can be as complex, as potentially dynamic, and as open to catharsis as the most shattering divorce. "It takes more courage to stay together," a friend once said to me, "than to go our separate ways."

We all know that a steadfast marriage can be dismantled in an afternoon, but how much is understood about the aesthetic light that such a revealed arrangement can produce? Long-term marriages do accrue a kind of compacted understanding, and there seems every reason to believe this material can be shaped to form a useful and novel dramatic arc, the prickly, conflicted spine of narrative fiction.

Perhaps it is this notion of conflict that needs revisiting; we may find that conflict is centered not in the fiber of human arrangements but in the interstices of human thought. What exactly are we owed? What can we aspire to? How well can we know another being? I'd like to begin over again—a project for the late nineties—asking why the rub of disunity strikes larger sparks than the rewards of accommodation, and how we've come to privilege what separates us above that which brings us together.

MEDITATIONS
ON DIVORCE

BY *Ellen Gilchrist*

I HAVE PUT this essay in the form of meditations because I do not have a theory to expound. I do not want to "lead you to an overwhelming question." All I have to offer are the ideas I have been entertaining for many years as I watched myself, my friends, and my children live through painful and troubled times in the courts of love. The higher the intelligence, the slower the rate of maturation. This is true in phylogeny, ontogeny, and in our lives. The more intelligent and sensitive the person, the more likely they seem to have their relationships end in chaos. Perhaps the intelligence and sensitivity make it more difficult for them to endure relationships that have gone bad.

Here are some of the things I have observed.

Divorce is caused by stupid marriages. By people getting married when they are too young or because they are scared or because they think a wife or husband will "complete" them. And divorce is often a very good idea. It's certainly better than a loveless or ill-suited or painful marriage.

Children are the victims of divorce. Most grown men and women go on to other relationships and, except for wasting energy being angry at the person they have divorced or been divorced by, usually manage to learn a little something from the interchange. Of course, unless they are in some sort of therapy during the marriage or divorce, they generally go on to repeat the cycle, hopefully with someone at least slightly more suited to their real needs (which very few people ever acknowledge or examine, much less try to overcome or alter). Between them, my two brothers have married five women who look like my mother. Blond, blue-eyed, polite, quiet, gentle, inflexible. But neither of my brothers is interested in talking about animas or in seeing patterns in their behavior.

Not that years of psychoanalysis have made a dent in my program. Every man I have been involved with has been the oldest son of a powerful woman. In the deep and meaningful relationships, the ones that ended in marriage, they have usually been the oldest son of three brothers. My father is the oldest of three brothers and the son of a powerful mother.

Perhaps it does no good to know any of this. Perhaps it is impossible to choose who we love or want to breed with. Still, for me, the ability to articulate and understand my experience makes up somewhat for whatever inconvenience I have been caused by my unconscious strivings and yearnings.

"We can do what we want, but we can't want what we want," a wise man wrote, and this is, alas, the long and short and the *halter* of it.

Why do we make these crazy marriages that end in tragedy or divorce? Because we have mothers. When we are born we are held against the soft skin of our mothers. (Unless we are unlucky and lose our mothers, but that is another story.)

This sets us up to fall in love. The minute you take off your clothes and lie down beside the soft skin of another human being, the relationship is changed forever. This is the ground of being. This is the big, big story. I have often thought, now that I am in my late middle age, a time surely of reflection and surmise, that perhaps we were better off with arranged marriages. To allow our young men and women to go off and lie down beside anyone they find attractive is dangerous. It often leads to marriages where the partners are unequal in money, scope, intelligence, sophistication, culture. These inequities are of no importance to nature, who wants us to breed far away from our DNA (hybrid vigor, that mother and father of beauty, genius, stamina, brilliance), but they are fertile ground for disagreement when the initial attraction begins to wane.

I have known many wise and wonderful men and women who were good at everything but staying married. Well-meaning men and women, who entered marriages with the best and purest of intentions, have been shocked and stricken to find they could not maintain the love they felt for the person they married, or, worse, that they fell in love with "someone new," as the language so brilliantly puts it. A marriage is altered by such yearnings whether the adulterous heart acts on them or not.

Even the best among us are subject to Cupid and his arrows, to our unconscious wishes to re-create and recast our childhood, to fall into romantic dreams that are doomed to fade and die and be repeated with new actors.

We reap what we sow. Divorce is the fruit of ignorance about our true nature. It is the harvest of ignorance. We cannot teach our children what we do not know. If we do not understand human sexuality and psychology, we cannot protect our young people from perpetuating the cycle of broken homes. We rush to buy our daughters elaborate wedding gowns and stage huge wedding parties. We feel like the bad fairy if we do not greet every engagement as a marvelous possibility, not to be questioned or probed. The minute two young people tell us they are getting married, we drop our judgment at the door and begin to ooh and aah.

IN THIS CULTURE of bad marriages, divorce is a good idea more often than it is a bad idea. But it is nearly always a bad idea for the children. The child nearly always sees it as a fault of his own. He thinks he has failed because his parents do not live together. He thinks he has not been good enough to deserve the American dream of an intact family. This seems to be true even when the lost parent was abusive or alcoholic. All around him the child sees images of families with both mothers and fathers, and it makes him feel impoverished if he has only half this loaf.

Perhaps there is nothing we can do about this. Perhaps we have to muddle along as we have been doing. Making messes of our lives and then cleaning them up as best we can.

YEARS AGO, Margaret Mead figured out a plan to lower our divorce rate and keep us from damaging our children. She posited a system of marriages. Any two grown people could apply for a license to be married or to cohabit. If the relationship was successful over a period of time, perhaps two to five years, then they could apply for a second license that would allow them to have a child together.

God knows, I do not want government meddling in the private lives of citizens, but at least we should try to teach young people not to have children until they have achieved a stable home. This means we must fight against nature. Nature doesn't care about quality. Nature has cast its lot with quantity.

The young people of the middle class who have access to reliable birth-control methods seem to be working out a system not unlike the one Margaret Mead proposed. They have a series of cohabitations, and, if one sticks for a long period of time, they get married and produce one or maybe two offspring. Sometimes these arrangements continue to work after the child is born. Sometimes they don't.

I HAVE THOUGHT about these matters for years, trying to understand my own failed marriages and the harm divorce wreaked on my sons. I took them away from their father and tried to keep them from him. I was so young I believed they belonged only to me. They had come from my body. I had risked my life to have them. It was impossible for me to think their father had any right to them. Now they are older and have divorces and broken homes of their own. Women have borne children for them and used the children to manipulate them. Women have taken their children from them and made them beg to see them. Because of this, they look at their father with new eyes and commiserate with him. I am glad that time and experience have partially healed a cruelty I thought I had a right to inflict.

I do not know how broken homes and divorces will be stopped. I know that knowledge is our only weapon. We must teach our children the history of our own divorces. We must warn them and beg them to be wiser than we were. We must do whatever is in our power to convince them not to marry until they are old enough to know themselves. How old is that? Thirty for some, forty for others, never for a few.

I AM ASKED all the time about how an artist can balance a family and work. And the truthful answer is that I do not know an artist of great or unusual talent who is married. I will revise that to say an artist of great or unusual talent who uses that talent fully. There is no room in the life of an artist for a husband or a wife or a normal family life. The hours an artist has to spend mulling around in solitude leave no time for the ordinary friendliness and courtesy that a happy marriage demands.

A happy marriage? I am so cynical I really cannot think of one. I know people who are married who have cut deals that allow them to live in relative peace with each other but I don't know any marriages that seem to be delivering much happiness. Perhaps marriage was never supposed to make us happy. Perhaps it is just the price we have to pay to reproduce and make a nest.

THE WORST THING about divorce is how long it takes to achieve it. It takes as long to decathect as it did to create the problem. For every romantic thought you had about the man or woman to whom you were married, you must now add a cynical, mean, ugly thought. For every time you decided he was Prince Charming, you must now decide he is Evil Incarnate. For every rapturous account of his virtues you gave your friends, you must now add a general account of his impossibility as a spouse.

Spouse: there's a word to make one shudder. From the term, espousal, which means to promise. For every ill-thought-out promise, you must add the legal fine print. Thank goodness for sofas and jointly owned automobiles. As soon as the argument can degenerate into a battle over property, the personal emotional ground can begin to be abandoned.

How ugly all this seems to us while we are going through it. How terrible we feel to be walking around thinking dark thoughts about someone we used to *sleep with*. Just when we think we are making some progress, we run into the person we are divorcing at the grocery store. "Ill met by moonlight, Proud Titania," Oberon says to his queen in Shakespeare's *A Midsummer-Night's Dream*. He has come upon her in the forest, where she is dancing with her fairies and elves. She has with her a young boy, the possession of whom is the cause of her dissension with Oberon. Their conversation begins with jealousy, moves on to Titania's blaming Oberon for everything that's wrong with the world, and ends with his throwing the blame back onto her. Especially with a subject as dark as divorce, it is good to stop and drink from the hands of a master.

TITANIA:
These are the forgeries of jealousy;
And never, since the middle summer's spring,
Met we on hill, in dale, forest, or mead,
By paved fountain or by rushy brook,
Or in the beached margent of the sea,
To dance our ringlets to the whistling wind,
But with thy brawls thou hast disturb'd our sport.

. . . .

The human mortals want their winter here;
No night is now with hymn or carol blest.
Therefore the moon (the governess of floods),
Pale in her anger, washes all the air,
That rheumatic diseases do abound.
And thorough this distemperature, we see
The seasons alter; hoary-headed frosts
Fall in the fresh lap of the crimson rose,
And on old Hiems' thin and icy crown,
An odorous chaplet of sweet summer buds
Is, as in mockery set; the spring, the summer,
The childing autumn, angry winter, change
Their wonted liveries; and the mazed world,
By their increase, now knows not which is which.
And this same progeny of evils comes
From our debate, from our dissension;
We are their parents and original.

Who has ever written a more perfect description of the way the injured party feels when a marriage has broken up? The winds have sucked up from the sea contagious fogs. Rivers have overborne their continents. The seasons have changed places. Hoary-headed frosts fall in the fresh lap of the crimson rose . . . And this same progeny of evils comes from our debate, from our dissension. . . .

by
ELLEN
GILCHRIST

S O M E T I M E S divorces are caused by children. Even a marriage that was consummated in the hope of having children may break down under the pressure of caring for and supporting the endless and expensive needs of children. Modern, educated women sometimes find the wear and tear of taking care of small children twenty-four hours a day is more than they bargained for.

I know of marriages that are breaking down because the children have become rebellious teenagers. The parents feel cheated. They have given their lives and the sweat of their brows for those ungrateful creatures. They feel they have wasted their lives. Perhaps they have.

Platitudes or shaky moral ground will not save us now. We have big problems in this culture. And all problems begin in infancy, in the home, in the mother-child relationship, and in the force field we call family.

Dustin Hoffman's brilliant portrayal of Captain Hook in the movie, *Hook,* is a lesson small children find easier to bear than most of the adults who see it. "They were happier before they had you," Hook tells the children. "They could do whatever they liked, without you always whining and asking for things."

Children know this is true. Why is it so hard for adults to admit it?

Some women make better mothers than others do. Some men make better fathers. This doesn't mean that some men and women are better than others, just that they are more temperamentally suited to the job of raising children. Where does this lead us?

One thing I know is that it is a bad idea to marry someone who had bad parents. If they hated their mother, if they were hated by their mother or father, your marriage will pay for it in ways both obvious and subtle. When the chips are down, when someone is sick or loses their job or gets scared, the old patterns will kick in and he will treat you the way he treated his mother or the way she treated him. If she yelled at him and compared him to others and blamed him for her own shortcomings, this is the treatment you will receive. If she expected to be constantly admired and rewarded, he will expect that. And this is just the problem with his (or her) mother. Before we even get to the father.

DIVORCES are also caused by people outgrowing each other or outgrowing the need for the marriage they have made. Sometimes marriages are broken down by events: the death or sickness of a child, the sickness or disability of one of the partners, sudden wealth, sudden poverty, all the things that the marriage ceremony in The Book of Common Prayer warned against. For richer, for poorer, for better, for worse, in sickness and in health, and forsaking all others . . .

The world that such marriages were made for no longer exists in the middle-class life of the United States. We *don't* depend on each other for food, clothing, housing, nursing, and are left depending on each other for company and emotional support. Most of the married people I know go to their friends for fun and gossip and long walks where everyone says exactly what they think.

Also, we live much longer than the people who wrote the ceremonies in the prayer books of our various religions. We don't want to forsake all others. We leave our troubled houses where children are sick and bills must be paid and travel to our offices where there are bright, well-dressed, good-natured people of the opposite sex, and we forsake. Oh, do we forsake! If not in physical ways, then in emotional ways, which are equally damaging to the marriages we left behind that morning.

W E L I V E so long we have time for two or three major careers, two or three or more transformations. We become someone new and the person we are married to feels betrayed. They have been betrayed. The person they married has ceased to exist and they feel cheated.

T H E O N L Y H O P E I can see for the unhappiness of divorce is knowing that it is better than a bad marriage. The unhappiness of divorce ends, in time, for healthy people. Healthy people refuse to stay unhappy. Sooner or later they wake up and decide to be happy again. They lose weight and start exercising. They dye their hair or get a toupee. They buy a red dress and go to a party and start flirting. They redecorate their living quarters. They get out their address books and start looking for old lovers to recycle.

Life goes on. They look back on their marriage and wonder who that person was who inhabited that troubled world. Time, the old healer, has erased the footsteps that led them to the altar and the divorce court.

THE
GENDER
WARS

BY *Diana Hume George*

$\mathcal{H}$E WAS the great love of my life—I always knew we'd grow old together—sacred territory—desecration fears—feels like betrayal to write this." So begin my notes for this essay, jotted on Post-its over many months. Reviewing the inch-thick pile, I find I'm still genuflecting three-fourths of an inch into it, lighting candles, saying novenas to him, to us: "I will always love him, even if we cannot be together. Finest man and mind I will ever know." It sounds more like an elegy than an anatomy of divorce. We believed our own press, idealized ourselves.

We had assistance mythologizing our relationship. When we broke up, many friends actually said some version of "You can't do this to us." We were one of those sparkling academic couples known by many people in our business. No wonder I write this sort of dribble on Post-its. I wrote the last note in the middle of the night in the dark, waking from another nightmare about him, one that left me vaguely nauseous throughout the next day. I can barely read the scribble, but I believe it says, "You stupid stupid man—infant—tyrant—grow up." I can't use his real name, so I'm going to call him Jason here, probably because he thought of me as a Medea, bent on destroying everyone I loved. Or maybe I was Medusa. Big hair.

I write about the breakup of my nearly twenty-year relationship from the perspective of a woman interested not only in telling a harrowing story about personal loss but also in figuring out how the story of my marriage intersects those of other women and men. I used to think ours was the greatest love the world had ever known, but I have come to see that we were enacting clichés, that the belief in our unique indissolubility was itself only a cliché. Had this been someone else's relationship instead of my own, I'd have known it all along.

Jason's perspective is diametrically opposed to mine. (His myth about himself is that he's always right. Mine is that I'm always reasonable.) Still, there are facts he would not dispute. He was once my professor and my mentor, although he did not believe that this influenced us to any significant degree. I saw a pattern of domination and submission in our relationship that he denied was there, and if he said it wasn't, then the subject wasn't up for discussion. He felt he'd changed quite enough as a male feminist and was not able to change any more. Though he ultimately agreed to counseling, he thought of it as "psychobabble." He believed that we should take care of our own problems rather than confiding them to a stranger and that talking about a problem was like digging into a wound and opening it further; I believed that bandaging a wound when it's festering only makes the infection worse.

I MET JASON in his poetry class in 1969. Although I was only twenty, I was married and a mother. I was immediately smitten by him—and by John Donne and the other poets whose words fell seductively, dramatically, from his lips. He was a charismatic professor, a consummate performer. Many of his women students fell for him.

I took so many classes from Jason that I lost count. For years, we called each other by our surnames, Dr. X and Ms. Y. My marriage fell apart. Later his began to crumble. Eventually he left his wife and family, and although I'd never been involved with a married man, I was way beyond the ability to pull myself back on the basis of my moral reservations. We fell into each other's arms one night. It wasn't all that romantic—we were in his office in the dark, and somehow my foot got jammed in the wastebasket. We told that story for years.

Our intensity and passion didn't wane with those years. Instead it grew steadily, taking us through losses and difficulties. His children and parents wouldn't speak to him; my first husband went to jail for a serious crime; my best friend's daughter ran away from home, came to live with us, and gave birth to a daughter at the age of seventeen. My son also became a parent. We were a family that included white, Native American, and black members—and in the small town where we lived that made us a target for bigotry.

Jason and I were never legally married; we were common-law for all those years. We were always in deep financial difficulty because of his child support payments and the low salary I earned as a graduate teaching assistant while working on my Ph.D. And lord, we were busy. He was a professor and activist with a commitment to union politics and affirmative action. I was a grad student and then a young professor with growing activist concerns in women's issues. We wrote books. Yet it wasn't these pressures that did us in. Throughout these years, we found ways to get away from the tension of our lives by traveling around the country in the summer, camping in a series of leaky tents. We determinedly saved at least one long afternoon a week, often more, for being together. We worked hard. We raised good kids. And we loved each other madly.

When the trouble began, it hit us unaware because we'd been so busy, but also because we'd begun to believe our own press as a golden couple who represented love triumphing over all odds. For my part, I'd known early on that despite the feminist convictions we shared, we'd been backsliding. It wasn't about groceries—he bought them. It wasn't about housework—he helped, though I did more than he. (We had one of those arrangements in which the man concentrates on repairs and taking out the garbage and hauling heavy stuff, while the woman does more of the daily chores.) And it wasn't about cooking— we traded off. It wasn't even really about child care—he was involved with the kids, taking them on trips out West, helping with homework. I dedicated much more time to child rearing than he did, feeling it appropriate since our son was my child from a previous marriage, and our adoptive daughter was my best friend's child.

I'm still trying to figure out what happened, and he's still trying not to. His best revenge was leaving me to figure things out alone. After almost twenty years of loving each other, we didn't have a single real conversation about what had gone wrong. I asked him repeatedly to talk with me. Repeatedly he refused. Since he wouldn't talk about it, I had to reconstruct the accident scene by myself, make up the other half of the dialogue we're never going to have.

Here is how I see it. From the beginning, we allowed dangerous elements to creep into our relationship, even when it was healthy and alive. Jason had tremendous personal authority, a big voice, an imposing physical presence. He was quick to anger and equally good at turning on the deep freeze. He didn't have to do any of this often—a few times a year was enough, because it was scary and you remembered it well and didn't want to cause it again. I learned early on not to cross him. It was just too dangerous.

I can't rightly blame Jason for trying to stonewall me, because it worked so well year after year. Wouldn't you try that method if it worked, if it saved you pain, if you could avoid personal conflict by shutting down challenge or dissent? For years I was afraid of displeasing him. When I finally got up the courage—and even from someone as self-possessed as I normally am, courage is the appropriate word here—to try to speak to him of power inequities, he'd say there weren't any, that we were complete equals. He would simply refuse to talk about it further. Period. Scared, I'd shut up again. For years at a time. Now, what makes a woman do that if she's a feminist and isn't being

85
⁓
by
DIANA
HUME
GEORGE

beaten and has analyzed traps such as this in literature and in the lives of her friends? I remain dumbfounded. I was writing feminist books on one hand, playing silenced daughter on the other.

Sex became an issue too. Remember the scene in *Annie Hall* with Diane Keaton and Woody Allen on either side of a split screen talking to their shrinks? "How often do you have sex?" the shrinks ask. The Woody Allen character answers, "Hardly ever, only three times a week." On the right, Keaton replies to the same question, "All the time, three times a week." Even the statistic matches Jason and me. Sometimes we'd laugh about that, but it was a deadly serious issue. My mother took DES, so I have chronic cervical problems. Sex was not always fun for me, and sometimes it was downright painful—if not at the moment, then afterward. It's stunning to me to recall how regularly both he and I expected me to put out. Amazing and unquestioned, that sense of entitlement on his part, loving duty on mine. Jason did not seem to understand that this young woman who had started out as his goddess of sex was all grown-up now, busy as hell, and sexually exhausted.

But I tried—it was the seventies and I believed that we were supposed to be liberated. We were supposed to lighten up. I lightened up. When we first got together, the agreement was that any time I didn't like what was happening, all I had to do was say so.

That's not what happened at all. What started out consensual became quietly, subtly coercive. He never forced me. There are ways other than physical force to get a person who loves you to do what you want. As I grew older, less daughterlike, less an acolyte and more my own person, certain things became unacceptable. But each time I would say I was having trouble with them, that they weren't okay anymore, he would withdraw from me, punishing me with unexplained coolness that he, of course, denied; but I couldn't help noticing that when I acted the part of his sex goddess again, everything became warm and fuzzy. The emotional price for not playing was high—although he never acknowledged that he was exacting it.

I have asked myself a hundred times: How did it come to the point where I lost the right to set reasonable limits and boundaries, to satisfy needs of my own? How can I reconcile the me I know—strong, autonomous—with the woman who was so silenced, so afraid? The process of self-erasure in a relationship happens in small, almost imperceptible increments, one isolated incident after another. There is always, in any human relationship, the decision to let it go for now, not to disturb the peace with this need or that hurt. When you let that silence build, a pattern of self-denial emerges. Because you have not said, *"Wait. We must talk now,"* you can lose the "right" to speak at all.

This happens to people in love all the time. Take away the specifically sexual focus, and we all can name a thousand ways it happens in our lives. It's so subtle, and there's so much background noise, that you don't even hear the sound of the handcuffs going click, and you didn't know that it was your own hands, raised to your beloved in this small submission, that were now bound.

Jason meant me no harm. I really believe that. He loved me. He was just a pained man living in a patriarchy he himself fought against, though he didn't understand its outposts in his own head. By the time I found the strength to meet his anger and disappointment with my own, mine was so concentrated from its long-term repression that it became destructive. Jason wouldn't discuss these issues, year upon year. Blue eyes gunning their warnings, he'd yell, "Go ahead and talk. I SAID GO AHEAD AND TALK. I'M LISTENING. SAY WHAT YOU HAVE TO SAY."

I finally found someone who would talk to me, who wanted to touch me in ways I did not find objectionable. Although he was no real threat to Jason in my eyes, Jason would say my affair caused our breakdown. We came completely undone.

I am fascinated by the way we remember, select, and devise "what happened" in a relationship, how we all rewrite the history of our lives, constructing our narratives so as to make ourselves whatever we want to be—heroes or martyrs or victims or visionaries. The "truth" about what happened at any given point in time recedes, or never existed to begin with, though it is enticing to behave as if there is a real "truth," a genuine, ultimately vindicating "what happened." On a bench somewhere in the universe sits a judge who can verify memories under dispute: She said what you remember she said; he turned from the table and put that piece of cake in his mouth and then sneered with contempt exactly as you recall; you behaved with long-suffering grace, and then with well-earned anger.

But of course, there is no such judge, which is why my truth and Jason's are mutually exclusive. Both of us are reasonable people and we were both *there*. Yet what he remembers is completely different from what I do.

Jason thinks that what happened is this. It's a script so simple and short that a gerbil could write it: He loved me completely and passionately and thought that I loved him back that way; whereas, flighty woman that I must have been all along in disguise, I got tired of him for some arbitrary reason—probably connected to my whacked-out midlife hormones—then betrayed him with another man, and finally just up and left him. Ninety-nine percent my fault. (Recent revision under pressure: "Sure, I made some mistakes." But no elaboration. None.) He said to our son that this mess was "all your mother's idea. She just left me." That's it. He omits the part where he actually told me to leave, at least a dozen times, before I finally went. And I left and came back more than once.

One of his most recent revisions of his own first draft includes a tub. Always eager for any little detail to illuminate what he thinks occurred and why, I listen close. "You just got up out of the tub and walked out the door," he tells me. "Tub? What tub?" "The bathtub," he answers, giving me his you-know-what-I'm-talking-about-don't-play-dumb look. It seems he was sitting next to the tub talking to me, and suddenly I rose up, swept past him, and walked out the door. I guess I dressed first.

Then I remembered: From my point of view, it was not a silent or unexplained departure, but a sad, resigned, talked-about one, even if I did more of the talking. It had happened the winter before our final breakup when I tried to leave for a few weeks to figure things out, but only managed to be gone for twenty-four days, during which I came back and slept at our house with him several days a week, got in a car accident with him, injured my leg; and then our dear old dog lost control of his body functions, so I gave it up and came back home completely. The dog died in my arms and Jason and I buried him together, strewing roses, weeping, holding each other, singing songs from the opera *Candide,* vowing to try again. I stayed for another six months, during which we tried to heal and could not. I had long since given up my affair and at Jason's demand was not even being civil to my former lover, which was very difficult. But by that time, Jason had introduced a new "family friend" into our home, the woman he later married, and with whom he was punishing me for my affair.

At that time, I felt so guilty and awful that I let him have her there, engaging in open physical affection right in front of me and our kids, cuddling our granddaughter to show off his good-daddy genes, and generally treating me like an irritating neighbor. Jason said he had to have her in his life because I did not love him like he loved me; she soothed the pain of my terrible withdrawal. I bought that crock all summer, comforting the grown kids when they cried, or reasoning with them when they begged me not to let this go on. Finally I left.

Yet according to Jason, the bathtub scene was the moment when I just walked out. What happened after that does not count. There's a gap in the narrative. I suspect that I, too, have engaged in similarly solipsistic narrative revisions, though I don't know what they are.

We'll never talk about it together. He'll be stuck forever in his simple martyrdom scenario about the man who gave all his love, his very life, to a woman who turned out to be—for no reason he could think of except perhaps racquetball hormones—a betraying liar who nearly destroyed him. He was the victim and I was the victimizer. Simple. But I wouldn't think a person could be content to let it rest with that. When the marriage of two complicated and decent people falls apart after two decades, it's not likely to be such a simple bad-girl–good-guy story.

We're trying to get on with our lives. He's married, I'm not. I doubt I ever will be again. Neither of us wants to keep hating the other. We share a history, two kids, two grandchildren. We can't always avoid each other. It's been over five years since we split. He doesn't speak ill of me to other people. That's called "loyalty," which he also demonstrates by being essentially uncommunicative about "what happened." It's a shame, he might say, but it's over, so it goes, what's done is done. How about those Cubs?

Yet to one or two close friends, he confided a whole different scenario in which I'm not a bad guy but a hormonal depressive. (Read long-suffering, painful toleration of mental illness on his part.) One of them told a third friend how sad it was: Poor Diana. All those years I never realized she was emotionally ill. She hid her instability so well. The third friend called to tell me that one. We had a good laugh.

I HAVE THOUGHT long and hard about why my marriage ended, and have tried to put it into a broader perspective, to understand how it conforms to certain patterns. One of these has to do with feminist marriages involving men who came to their equity politics in the women's movement of the early 1970s, adopting a conscious program of personal growth and transformation. Such men formed their deeply held beliefs during adulthood, long after the massive machinery of gender construction had done its work in the unconscious. They constitute a socially, economically, and educationally advantaged elite. These men entered into marriages with women of my generation on a basis of equality—striven toward, strenuously maintained. They're the good guys.

Surely many feminist marriages are exactly what they appear to be—successful partnerships between a man and a woman who live together in mutual recognition, respect, and carefulness. But judging from my own personal sampling, the country must be fairly crawling with women who have lived a weird double life for years, or are living it still, maintaining the fiction that they are in genuinely feminist marriages, when both husband and wife have long since backslid. Women in marriages such as this often take part in creating the myth that theirs are partnerships of equality (I certainly did), when they know deep down, and often say to their closest friends, that most of the change and transformation have been their own, that their men sometimes treat them with contempt and expect from them an enormously draining kind of dedication that is not fully mutual.

A great many feminist men are also misogynists *because of their feminism*. Such men often feel deep if suppressed anger over what they gave up when they relinquished privileges that would otherwise have been theirs. And in some feminist men this rage is directed toward women. If you get in the way of it, you can be in big trouble.

It has also struck me how my relationship with Jason contradicted gender clichés. In our culture, women are thought to be emotionally needy and vulnerable and more dependent on relationships for their identities than men. Research on female psychology supporting these generalizations cannot be all wrong. But has anyone out there noticed what my friends and I most certainly have? That many middle-class men in their forties and older seem to be more emotionally dependent than their women? Am I making this up? Why are the women I know forever getting up from the dinner tables of their lives, from precious moments with their women friends, because *he* is waiting? Because he can't get to sleep without her? Because he needs her near him? Because he feels abandoned if she's gone too long?

It's no secret that many men dump older wives in midlife and take up with younger women. Indeed it seems to me epidemic, especially among men in positions of power in business, the arts, politics, and — like Jason — academia. I was one of the younger women on an older man's arm. I was Jason's midlife crisis. Men like him are mentor figures — younger women's bosses or superiors or teachers — and old patterns of domination and submission, of desire to please daddy, die hard. It's thought that father/daughter, domination/submission patterns exist even in normative heterosexual love when the man and woman are relatively the same age. When a man is a woman's senior, the difficulties of the norm become exaggerated. Partnering with a patriarch can be hazardous.

What is more, recent research on female psychology and moral development indicates that men tend to place a high value on hierarchy, autonomy, and authority, and don't appear to care as much about empathy or the perspectives of others as women do. There are exceptions, of course, but it's common for men to believe so deeply in their rightness, and to have so much difficulty admitting they might be wrong, that they often cannot take their share of the responsibility for failed relationships. Women, on the other hand, are normally enculturated to believe that nurturing relationships is their deepest obligation, and tend to internalize responsibility and guilt when relationships fail. In effect, the tendency is for men to say, "It's all your fault, you did it" and for women to reply, at least initially, "You're right. What a worthless human being I am." It's a tidy arrangement, but I can't imagine that it's good for our long-term chances as people trying to make it together on a fragile planet.

Beyond this, I've noticed that men are less likely than women to enter into marriage counseling, which by definition involves compromise. When pushed to do so, they often engage in the process with little real desire to change their own patterns of behavior, feeling on a basic level that it's only the women who *really* need to change or grow, so the process never has a chance.

We live in a patriarchy. Men have more power than women do, and many men have trouble sharing that power. Capitulation to authority is a major pitfall for women; the ability to be flexible and to change may typically come harder to men. We can all name exceptions — rigid and always-right women, empathic men — but they don't disturb the rule.

JASON BELIEVES I hate men. But I don't think this is true. I am sometimes afraid of men, and sometimes, in anger, I make sweeping generalizations I know aren't entirely true. But I like most men I know. And as a teacher of women's studies, I understand how both sexes have been shaped by the patriarchy.

Jason believes he does not harbor any significant misogyny. It's not a danger in his mind, so he doesn't challenge or examine himself. Like many feminist men, he represses his anger at women, regarding it as inadmissible. Still, he has expressed his rage in both words and action, including fits of temper. He is a powerful man who has identified with the causes of oppressed peoples and fought for their rights for many years—and in some respects, beyond his conscious intentions, I think he resents them for it. He'd probably say that I simply drove him beyond the ability to cope—i.e., that a man can only stand so much.

He is now married to a woman even younger than I am. If I was almost young enough to be his daughter, she's almost young enough to be his granddaughter. But he would say this has nothing whatsoever to do with his need for a younger woman. She was "there to love me when you nearly destroyed me," he once told me. I have other interpretations, knowing that he desired me in part because he could make me his projection of a goddess of sexuality with whom he might regain his own sense of youth. It is no coincidence that he is yet again with a woman in her twenties, approximately the age I was when I first came to him. He needs the kind of love the young give their elders. He got it from me, too. I don't hold myself above that dynamic, which possesses its seductions and its beauties.

WHAT DOES it matter if Jason and I never figure out what really happened between us? I believe it matters; men and women need to come to some mutual understanding of what happened to them, how they damaged each other and themselves, what they might have done to avert their tragedies, might still do to avert the next one. I think Jason and I misunderstood each others' motives and intentions. In order that our time together should not be written off as wasted—making us bitter and wary of other loves—we need to know what happened.

But now that we are separated, neither of us can understand anything beyond isolated, self-serving truths—and to me that feels horribly dangerous. If a man and woman who both care about a world larger than their own conflicts cannot make the effort to understand each other—or at least to listen to each other now that there is no primary relationship left to save, no flanks to protect—then what hope is there for peace and understanding in a broader context? Global conflict is personal conflict writ large.

If all I wanted was female martyrdom, aggrieved party status, support for not only my valid perceptions but also for my inevitable self-deceptions, then all I'd have to do is—well, nothing at all. I've gotten plenty of sympathy and confirmation of my version of reality from my friends. But I want something more, something better. I will always want to know what Jason experienced and felt. I want to understand what he was going through, now that I can see beyond my own pain. I want to take responsibility for the parts of this that belong to me. I can't really know what they are when he says it was *all* my fault, because that only makes me strike back defensively, or conclude that the fault was really all his. Neither of us can possibly be right about that.

The man I began living with a year after Jason and I separated was with me for several years. I chose him in part because he seemed to be the kind of person who could do what Jason could not—tear down with me, brick by brick, the walls that rise between people entangled in love. He said he could do it, but finally he could not. When I said it was time to go our separate ways, he, too, decided it was all my fault. He was my victim. I was malicious. I abused him terribly. Like Jason, whose opposite he claimed to be, he will not talk to me about why our relationship ended. Like Jason, he says that perhaps he did make a mistake or two, though he does not say what they were. Still, he is glad to provide elaborate details on what I did wrong, which, apparently, was just about everything.

I know that none of us, male or female, can erase our unconscious drives. Our desires and needs were instilled in us early and are difficult to dislodge. But what I am desperately weary of is what I have always encountered in my personal relationships. It is not men's birthright to ask of women that we set no boundaries. It is not right that men's agendas, expectations, and needs so often become definitive of love relationships. It may be harder for men in a patriarchy to understand their limits, their relative powerlessness, and sometimes it may be almost impossible for them not to blame women for their defeats. I want them to try harder. Female conditioning may give some women an advantage—ironic as it is—in that they learn to be better at handling defeat and compromise. I know I cannot re-create myself to conform to a lover's image of me—and I am resigned, now, that the men I love cannot re-create themselves for me. I just hope that someday I will encounter a man who will take responsibility with me for whatever losses and pains we must endure together. In the meantime I'm taking a break from the gender wars.

GROUNDS

BY *Mary Morris*

A FEW MONTHS AGO I was standing in New York's Penn Station en route to Washington to visit a friend. It was a Friday afternoon and the station was crowded. Other travelers bustled about. Trains were announced and I listened to the various "All aboards" that rang through the station. When my train was called and I looked down, my leather backpack was gone.

The backpack contained student papers, a novel I was reading, my journal, some notes for stories. It also held my checkbook, credit cards, the keys to our house, my address book with all kinds of numbers, codes, secrets. All the things you aren't supposed to carry. In a panic I phoned my husband and told him to call the banks, the brokers, the creditors, the locksmith. Freeze the mortgage account, change our PINS. We had to cancel, stop everything.

I will spare you the logistical difficulties this produced: the deposits that disappeared into dead accounts, the changing of keys, the thirty-five checks my husband wrote on an account we had shut. What we had to open, what we had to close. But in the midst of a long, tedious bank session, I turned to my husband of five years and told him that now I knew I could never get divorced. I couldn't stand the paperwork.

First let me say that I have never been divorced, not legally. Not with documents, papers to file, custody battles, accounts to separate, not to mention books and records. I have never had to fiscally and on the dotted line divide myself from another. But I have suffered rifts, splits, separations, and breakups. I have lost a friendship that meant more to me than any friendship should. Most relevant to this essay, I've had to wrench myself away from a man with whom I'd spent several years, had a child, as well as assorted emotional ties. This must count for something. I have had to pick up the pieces, pull myself together, and begin a new life with an infant daughter.

When she was two, I married someone else, a jewel of a man, a gift, one of my closest friends said. He has adopted our daughter, Kate. We have a house, a dog, many records, and books and CDs and dishes and even some fine crystal and an antique bed we are both very attached to and rosebushes we love to prune and, of course, all that paperwork in common. Our books are merged into one good-sized library. Though we know this is conventional, I make the child-care arrangements and he pays the bills. We like the same movies and people and always order pad thai at our favorite Thai restaurant around the corner.

Yet every day I think to myself, this is it. I'm going to get divorced. I can't spend another minute with this man. I can't bear the way he scrubs the pots with those long tedious strokes, the way he walks the dog, always wary of letting it off the leash. I can't stand how he shifts his leg just when I'm cuddled in the right position. The way he puts things on the top shelf where he knows I can't reach. He does dumb things. Breaks the window of the hatchback before we leave on a vacation. Loses his keys. Hides the butter in the back of the fridge. I can't stand the pauses between sentences, the way silence sometimes creeps in between the cracks.

I know I am not fit for this marriage, any more than a stallion is fit for the corral. Orcas may swim in pods, but on the open sea. I can't live any longer in this cage, this trap. This accountability. I want to be able to walk out the door and not say that I'm going to the store and I'll be back in an hour. I don't want to phone in if I am late or apologize if something takes longer than it should. I don't want someone reading my thoughts or, worse, not reading them.

I used to be a drifter. I traveled where I wanted, when I wanted. For a year and a half I roamed through Central America and didn't tell anyone where I was. I crossed Siberia and no one knew how to reach me. Now, if I sneak out through my studio door, panic ensues. Wherever I am, like E. T., I have to phone home. I've come to admire the great escape artists—Houdini; the prisoners who swam away from Alcatraz; the distant cousin of mine who kissed his wife good-bye, got on his usual train, and was never heard from again. I am in awe of the ones who got away.

I have thoughts of moving west. Or east. Of packing up and starting over. Once I tried this. When I told my daughter's biological father that I thought we should make it legal, he said, "In what sense?" Since he is a professor of international law, I assumed he knew what legal meant. I decided that I needed to find a new place and begin again. I also needed a job because the same year Kate was born I lost mine, and there was one I could have in California. I packed up my daughter and headed to the other coast to start afresh.

As soon as I stood beneath the statue of the Duke at John Wayne International Airport, I knew I'd made the mistake of my life. There is a great tradition of people who moved to California to start over. A whole body of literature is dedicated to this theme, such as *Grapes of Wrath* or *Day of the Locust*. There is also another interesting motif that runs through California literature—deaths on the Pacific Coast Highway, car crashes, vehicles sailing over the edge. There is, after all, no place to go from there. It's the end of the line.

IN CALIFORNIA I lived in a house that overlooked the sea and every day as I walked my baby along the cliffs, I thought to myself, "I could just jump off and end it all here." I had no friends, no one to turn to. But, of course, as I watched the water battering the rocks, I knew that I couldn't leave my child behind because who would care for her? and I couldn't take her with me because even in my despair such selfishness was not an option.

I had no choice. I had to live. Besides, her father and I had not had to separate our books or our finances. It was simply a divorce of the heart, one I was very slow in making. Nothing was made final between us. We were apart, that was all. I'd walk the cliffs weeping. Then return home to black smoke pouring out the window because Ramona, the woman I'd hired to help with the baby, left pots burning on the stove.

Mornings I hiked. Endless pacings back and forth through the hills above my house, baby on my back. There were mountain lions, coyotes, snakes up there. I took risks I shouldn't have taken. There were also butterflies, and Kate called them "Bye-byes." I should listen to her, I thought.

Because I had a baby and an automobile, two things I'd never had before, I began to drive. Through a series of strange events and journalistic curiosity, I became interested in coping. I infiltrated the California New Age groups and met with channelers, extraterrestrial walk-ins, goddesses, psychics, people who had been abducted by UFOs. I drove with my daughter all over Southern California, into the desert. Near the Nevada border we'd stop at chapels where we'd spend the afternoon watching people get married. Most of them had met the night before in Las Vegas and they all got in the car and headed west.

From pay phones in the middle of desert towns, I'd phone Kate's father. I'd tell him I wanted to get married. I'd tell him I loved him and we should try again. He said to be patient, to wait. He had finances to settle, his sons needed to grow. He would accept more responsibility soon.

One afternoon I drove to the Crystal Cathedral where, posing as a *New York Times* reporter, I interviewed the angels who flew in their pageants—grown women in pink gossamer who flapped their wings forty feet in the air. Each angel had her story—divorce, betrayal, loss. And as Peter Pan's riggers flew me through the cathedral, too, I understood that if you don't flap, you flip.

I wanted to fly, to soar, but somehow I couldn't break away. He called. He visited. We went to Death Valley (no symbolism intended) for Christmas. We fought. Why not just say yes? I'd argue. Why not just try? At night we lay side by side, hardly touching. We tried to patch it up, not just the fight, but the whole thing. I wanted him to sell his house where he'd lived with his previous family and make a fresh start with ours. On New Year's Eve a woman phoned him, just after twelve. I told him to leave. He said he barely knew her. We patched it up again. He said he did want to try so we made Valentine's plans. He broke them. He said he'd promised his sons he'd take them skiing and could I fly from Orange County to Burlington, Vermont, with the baby for the weekend? Every night we talked. Long, painful conversations until at last we agreed. We would try again. Perhaps he could handle the responsibility. He loved us. "You are the sea in which I swim," he said. He wanted us. His life was complicated. Life was full of complexities. We would meet. Neutral territory. Florida where my parents have a place (relatively neutral anyway). He would bring his boys. I'd bring our daughter. I was stupid, everyone said. But I loved him. We would try again.

"ONLY CONNECT," E. M. Forster wrote in *Howards End.* I was in graduate school when I read that, and it has stayed with me. Only connect. I know that longing and desire — and that need to make contact — are what keep fiction and life moving.

I have had this recurrent dream. That I am in a deep, dark hole. Words are my only way out. I keep trying to make the connections over and over again.

We talked. All the time. Our relationship was one endless dialogue, the same story told over and over again. Conversation is the erotic center of marriage, Dalma Heyn suggests in her book, *The Erotic Silence of the American Wife*. It is talk, dialogue, language that keeps us going. But in my case that talk was filled with cunning, deceit, betrayal. Perhaps because I am a writer, I was slow to see. Words are not actions, not really, when it comes to marriage.

AFTER WEEKS of negotiating, Kate's father and I met in Florida, our neutral ground. I had not seen him in three months. He stood, flanked by his teenage sons, and I had our daughter in my arms. He looked very good to me. *What is wrong with this picture?* I asked myself. I was never very adept at that test in school, but now I wracked my brain. When you live with somebody, when you know them for years, you get to know their quirks. He won't eat oatmeal, hates crowds, and prides himself in not having been to a barber in over twenty-five years. I had cut his hair for the past five years. His ex-wife for seventeen years before that.

Now I looked at him. His trimmed hair and beard. I took a step back and remembered the voice of that woman on the phone New Year's Eve. "Who cut your hair?" I asked him. "Who cut your hair?"

———

JOYCE CAROL OATES writes in *On Boxing* that the boxer, like the writer, is always reestablishing the parameters of self. Many times I have had to reestablish my parameters, regroup, circle my wagons.

For example, I have asked my husband, if I put my book down at night and gaze dreamily into space, not to say to me, "What are you thinking?" Of course he views this as a double bind—only connect, but leave me alone. I say, "I'll tell you what I'm thinking if I want to," but I also think, "You let me go, you let me fall back down into that deep, dark hole."

He says this is a paradox. My hands are tied.

And I say I am reestablishing my parameters. I'm trying to get back in the ring.

I MARRIED my husband because the Navajo Tribal Police were going to arrest us for driving what they thought was a stolen vehicle (my brother's van) and found out that Larry was a Canadian living in the U.S. on an expired tourist visa. Three weeks later, we married out of fear of deportation. We also married because when I put my head on his chest, I could fall asleep. Because when I phoned him, he was where he said he'd be. Because life felt easier, not harder, when he was there, and when I talked, he listened.

Just before our wedding, my husband came to the marital suite and I handed him my wedding shoes. I need you to scuff these, I said. His best man was with him and they walked around Plymouth Court in Chicago each with one of my shoes in their hands, scraping the soles on the asphalt so I wouldn't slip on the rug.

As I waited alone in our bridal suite, I thought of my father's words: You can always correct a mistake; that's what divorce courts are for. Or Jeanette Winterson's about marriage being a plate-glass window and someone's always standing outside with a rock.

WHAT ENABLED me to leave one man and love another, I'll never know. Sheer force of will, the need to fly, my daughter's happiness. Something between a mother's strength as she lifts the car off her child and the delicacy of a hummingbird's heart prevailed. I met someone new. En route to our wedding, we stopped at Arcosanti, that utopian village in the Arizona desert. An announcement on the bulletin board said that the great minds of the twentieth century would be visiting and I saw a picture of Kate's father. I took a deep breath; I went on with my life. Love is never the same and no one replaces another.

After years of rifts, breakups, separations, and now marriage, I know that there are no fresh starts. There are only new problems. Perhaps one can avoid messy divorce (one can even avoid marriage and commitment as I did for years). Certainly one can make a mistake and marry the wrong person and find an easy or not-so-easy way out, but the truth of it all is you don't start again. Life is cumulative—both happiness and grief. You drag it behind you. It piles up in the attic. Other people notice. I also know that things tend to happen for the best.

Another man might not shift his leg when I've found just the right position, but he also might not come home when he says he's going to. He might let the dog off the leash, but he might talk on the phone in whispers and not say where he's been. He might break my heart, or worse, my daughter's.

What's that movie with Ray Milland when the daughter cries to her parents that they can't know what she's suffering in love because they've always been in love and had such a perfect life? And they stand up and say, Do you know how many times I've thought about leaving him, how many times I've wanted to walk out on her? Marriage is work, my father always said. Just like anything else.

Years ago when I was a child, we got a flat tire. A man stopped to change it. It began to rain and that man lay on his back on the wet ground, whistling, changing the tire and explaining to me what he was doing. Later my mother said, "When you grow up, if you meet a man who can change a tire in the rain, whistle, and talk to a kid, marry him."

FOR YEARS I wrote short stories. I liked them better. Then I turned to novels. It became obvious to me right away that a short story was a fling and a novel was a marriage. A short story could happen on a two-week vacation, a brilliant passion that was soon over. But a novel was something you got up with every day. It was daily life, a process. Some days are good, some are bad, but you watch it build, slowly, over the years.

This is why I won't divorce my husband. Because while I take a shower, he makes the coffee. While he takes a shower, I get our daughter dressed. Because we dislike the same people and neither of us can put up a tent, nor wants to. Because when we walk down the street in a city where we've never been, he sees the light shimmering on the buildings. Because in the face of an injustice, he will rant and rave. I always know where he is. I know when he will call. He has never disappointed me in any way that matters. Because the mystery of love remains a mystery to me and when he lies down beside me, I know I can sleep.

Because I'm the kite and he's the string. Because I can't stand the paperwork. Because he'll read this essay and laugh.

When I tell my husband I've got grounds, he thinks I mean coffee grounds for the compost, not grounds for divorce. And most of the time he's right.

THE

DIVORCES

OF OTHERS

BY *Perri Klass*

*W*HEN MY SON started at the day-care center, he met other babies, just as interested as he was in Cheerios and Jolly Jumpers. And I, of course, met the parents. Fair is fair; a peer group for the child, a peer group for the parents. All those I-can't-believe-I'm-really-having-this-conversation conversations that you can only have with people who have children the same age as yours, from Competitive Motor Achievements ("Well, yes, he does pull himself up to a standing position all the time, he just seems so eager to walk") to Toilet Training Tips (don't ask). And the way you report back at home, as if it were interesting gossip, the details of other families, other ways of raising children: "She still hasn't ever let him have anything with sugar in it!" "They play foreign language tapes while the baby is sleeping—they think she'll absorb French pronunciation!" "They're leaving the kids with their housekeeper and going to Puerto Rico for the weekend!"

This is what we had, I suppose, instead of gossip. I have spent my life as a busybody and a gossip, and enjoyed a hundred vicarious personal dilemmas for each one that has actually unsettled my own somewhat tediously straightforward life. I have depended on friends and on the stories of friends of friends for a great many tortured love affairs and tumultuous passions, splendid acts of reckless abandon, and minor delicious perversities. All through high school and college and medical school, I drew interest and inspiration, tension and titillation, from the varying promiscuities and entanglements of my peer group.

But now I had landed on a plateau, a stage in life where there were no unexpected roughnesses in the landscape. No interesting gossip. Occasionally, I would call a friend who was single and childless, or lurching from relationship to relationship. "Tell me what's new," I would beg. But my friends got married and coupled off. "How are Larry and the baby?" they would ask, and confide that they were thinking of getting pregnant someday soon. Life became rather remarkably wholesome and familial on every side, and I grew increasingly desperate for dirt; I cannot speak for anyone else, but I know that I have never bought and read *People* magazine more faithfully than I did during those years.

And then came divorce. And though I have never been divorced, and for that matter, have never even been married, I found myself watching and discussing the divorces of others with various shades of fascination, titillation, and perturbation. Divorce, I suppose, comes to represent some large and dangerous whirlpool at the center of the calm, mature (and occasionally monotonous) sea of domesticity-with-young-children. It's there, it's a hazard, you can only give thanks that you've escaped—but it makes for intriguing conversation and occasionally you find yourself venturing a little closer just to get a better look.

These, after all, are the people who could so easily be you, the people you have been identifying with for years. Parents talk all the time about peer groups and developmental stages, and they are generally referring to their children. But one unexpected aspect of childbearing, unexpected for me at least, is that having a child also generates for parents a set of people united by their similarly aged children, and drawn behind those children through a set of developmental stages in the unfolding of a family. In my circle, it turned out, divorce tends to come when the second child is preschool-aged. Call it some variant of the seven-year itch, call it the compound stress of life with two young children, but I have seen few, if any, one-child divorces from up close. The family breakups in my day-care center followed a definite and distinct pattern. Couples had one child, then another, usually two or three years apart, and then, when the second child was not yet in kindergarten, came the divorce.

And the divorces were ugly. Suddenly, I knew the names of local divorce lawyers: who's really easy to talk to, who's not too expensive because she's still getting established, who's the big-money power divorce lawyer—why, he won't even take your case unless he thinks it's a really hot one. But if he takes it, your spouse might as well give up right away. Everyone learned the new vocabulary:

the guardian ad litem thinks . . . temporary primary custody . . . joint physical custody.

Sometimes the day-care center would get involved in the custody battle; teachers would be called on to testify which parent picked up and dropped off. The not-divorcing (or, if you prefer, not-yet-divorcing) among the parents would whisper to one another, did you know, they subpoena the pediatrician to find out which parent brings the kids when they're sick! And not-yet-divorcing couples would look at each other narrow-eyed: ah-ha! I would mutter to Larry, who believes that because I am a doctor myself, I am the one best equipped to deal with our pediatrician. Take that! You might be sorry someday that you made *me* call the doctor that time *you* saw the funny-looking poop!

It was often strange and sad and even terrible to watch families come apart, families that were in some sense mirror images of my own—and yet, terribly enough, there was also wrapped up in all the sadness some small element of excitement, of change and possibility. No, this place we have come to, this plateau of family life, is not necessarily where we rest forever. There is still the possibility of drama and tragedy and metamorphosis; new conformations, new households taking shape. It is sad and frightening to learn that promises of forever are not necessarily about forever—and yet it can be slightly intoxicating to wonder, for perhaps the first time in years, whether you really do know for absolute sure the shape of your own life in the years to come. What if, what if—what if you broke your own promises? What if he broke his? What if the small irritations and exasperations of daily life multiplied and ultimately imploded? Oh, I clucked over the divorcing couples, shook my head about the effects on their children, participated in the general pleasurable buzz of rising gossip—but there were moments too, I think, when I looked at those parents with fascination and fear, wondering whether I was just watching the bravest pioneers, the first to march boldly down a perilous path which would ultimately beckon many of those self-satisfied uxorious cluckers.

And yes, indeed, suddenly there was gossip. I had single, sexually active friends, who called and wanted the latest on my day-care center scandals. At the day-care center, I would scrutinize other parents for signs of personal change. A new haircut, a new clothing style—could it mean something? At pick-up time, you could, if you had the right kind of mind, hang around in the parking lot a little, letting your child say a slow good-bye to a good friend, and watch to see which parent of an acrimonious couple was doing the picking up, check to see if some mysterious stranger was waiting in the car. You could rush on home and tell the news: Karen got her hair cut short and curled and there was a guy waiting for her at pick-up time—in a silver Mercedes!

The divorces, I think, pushed many parents into overacting their roles. The still-happily-married-and-proud-of-it would nuzzle a little in the corridors, stagger out to their cars while attempting to embrace both each other and the cherished child: See how we love each other, see how tight and definite is our nuclear family! The recently-divorced-and-aware-of-the-scrutiny-of-others would parade defiantly past the cubbies in newly short skirts or unaccustomed contact lenses: I feel ten years younger and I know I've never looked better, and see how my child runs to hug and kiss me! Instead of merely reacting to one another's styles of child-rearing, many parents were making larger, more global statements. There was: I keep my promises; I love my wife, my husband, my child; I am a good and honorable person with a stable family. And there was, also: Stability is not everything; good and honorable people do not always know what's around the next corner; I also love my child; *life is more complicated than you think.* Yes, I definitely had a sense, looking at those parents who were living through divorces, that they were the wiser ones, the ones who had learned the hard lessons that others were still trying to avoid, lessons about the sadness and uncertainty of life and the limitations of security.

I spent a day at the courthouse with a friend, offering support and my own wisecracking variety of comfort as she plowed through another stage in a particularly angry and difficult divorce. What I remember most about that day was the matter-of-fact parade of family fights, one after another, as we sat waiting our turn. The court-appointed guardians, the lawyers who all knew one another, the bustle in the courthouse halls. The estranged husbands and wives aware of each other's presence, meeting glances defiantly or avoiding one another's eyes. It was the other side of gossip, the institutionalization of emotion and human connection, the professional pawing over and sorting out of human complexity. Life is more complicated than you think.

And then I went home and even in private felt polarized into that extreme of demonstrative we-are-a-stable-couple-aren't-we overacting. This will never happen to us, will it? We will never join that parade, will we? No, no, no. We are different, you promise each other, and promise it more fervently the less clearly you see the differences. In the end, we always fell back on the not-funny joke: We aren't married so we can't get divorced. Ha ha ha.

And then came the divorce that rocked the day-care center. Not another case of they-just-weren't-getting-along, not another she-says-he-has-somebody-else, not even she-got-a-better-job-out-of-state-and-he-says-he-doesn't-want-to-go. No, this was the grand passion of the four-year-olds' room: One little girl's mother and another little girl's father! Right there, in our day-care center, illicit passion! Adulterous love! Endless rumors flew: How long has this been going on and where did they meet and who found out when and who said what when who said which.

Now *this* was gossip, and with a vengeance. And it was vicarious thrills of many kinds: This too can still happen in families with young children, attraction too strong to re-sist, passion which carries away all before it, the world well-lost for love, and so on. There was intense disap-proval, there was pity for the abandoned spouses (which became more complicated when the husband whose wife had left him moved in with the mother of yet another four-year-old in the same day-care room—but that's an-other story), there was intense interest in the unfolding drama. And I suppose there was also some complicated half-resentful envy, the envy of those whose lives seem to have lost all gossip value, and even any possibility of gossip value in the future. As you picked up your child, argued the winter boots on, and remembered the lunch box and the accumulated artwork, you could not help wondering, in some tiny base corner of your being, whether someday you too might be a public scandal. Yes, even this is pos-sible, even for those grown well past adolescence, even for those fully equipped with children and highchairs and car seats and lunch boxes.

I remember a day spent on the beach the summer before my second child was due to start that same four-year-old room, Larry and I and another day-care center couple. The children were burying one another in the sand, fighting over the waterguns, and generally carrying on; the parents were conducting a symposium: Which marriages will break up this year? Present company was, of course, excluded from consideration; we did successfully finger one couple who went on to have serious (and public) domestic problems over the course of the coming year, but they didn't actually separate. We worked ourselves up into crude hysterics imagining unlikely adulterous pairings among the parents — Jack's buxom loudmouthed mother and Leah's tiny little buttoned-up father. We imagined ourselves giving testimony against particularly disliked and self-righteous parents. But present company was of course excluded; no matter how well we might fit the profile (second child now preschool-aged), obviously we were all looking down on the foibles of our fellow parents from some lofty peak of secure couplehood.

My son is in the fifth grade now, and divorce has finally penetrated his consciousness. I found it fascinating that when he was younger, he didn't seem to notice that one good friend's father was now living with another friend's mother — the adult personae had changed radically, but I couldn't help wondering whether to four-year-old boys, all adults looked more or less alike. In my more paranoid moments, I wondered whether he could pick me out of a line-up. But now that he's older, he's aware that certain friends of his have complex home lives—you can't usually see Danny on the weekend, because he goes to his father and stepmother, and they live a long distance away; if you want a sleepover with Greg, it has to be one of the two weekends a month that he's at his father's house, and it has to be there, not here, because his father doesn't want to lose one of his nights. Inevitably, one day, after an involved school vacation visit with Danny (pick up from mother, drop off at father—no, there's been a change of plan, but mother and father are not communicating directly, and all calls are funneled through stepmother), my son got disproportionately upset over a routine parental squabble in his own home.

"I don't want you to get a divorce," he said, and I had the feeling that he was trying on the drama for size, that this was less a sincere statement of loving anxiety than an attempt to say something about Danny and adults and the way they can mess up your life.

We won't, I said. We can't get a divorce, anyway—we aren't married. Ha ha ha. Look, you know me, I yell at everyone all the time and it doesn't mean anything. Look, I said, we love each other, we love you, and we'll stay together, even if we fight sometimes.

There are so many interesting promises, spoken and unspoken, that you make when you raise children. Some are the out-and-out impossible promises that you make even though they are not in your power: I won't die until you're all grown-up, nothing bad will happen in the night, I will protect you, always and forever. Some are the promises that seem reasonable and plausible, seem like they *should* be in your power: I will never hurt you, I will provide for you, our family will stay together. You don't stop making these promises just because you know that they, too, are not real promises, are only hopes and resolutions and small defiant plantings of the flag in what may be uncertain ground.

I make no apologies for relishing the details of other couples' marital discordancies, from the Prince and Princess of Wales to the parents at my children's elementary school. Yes, every fall when the school puts out the directory of parents' names and addresses, I still pore over it to see who has moved out on whom, who has dropped her husband's name off the end of the hyphen, who has remarried and now lists a stepparent. But I no longer speak from that lofty peak of secure couplehood, that above-it-all vantage point of amused distance. The lessons of my peer group, as we march through life, labeling our children's sweatshirts and signing up for teacher conferences, are in part lessons of complexity and vulnerability, the failure of good intentions, the transience of what was supposed to be permanent. They are also lessons of change and transformation and possibility, renewal and surprise. Adulthood and parenthood are not necessarily the known, safe quantities you thought they were, not for you and not for anyone else. Whether it is a warning or a titillation, a distant naughty frisson or a genuinely frightening premonition, you have to face the fact: Life is more complicated than you think.

IT'S

A WONDERFUL

DIVORCE

BY *Ann Hood*

$\mathcal{S}$HORTLY AFTER my divorce, I went to a psychic. He spread tarot cards on the table between us, studied them, and frowned.

"Recently," he said, "you lost a piece of jewelry."

I shook my head. I am not much of a jewelry wearer. In fact, I wore the same pair of earrings every day for three years until one literally fell off my ear.

The psychic continued my reading. I was in the arts, I was in financial ruin, I would move soon.

"Then there's that jewelry you lost," he said again. "The funny thing is, you're glad you lost it."

I thought about the jewelry box that sat on my bureau. It had been a gift from my ex-husband. Every year, on our anniversary, he gave me a box of some kind: one that played music; one that was made of glass; a painted ceramic one; and the large, square, wooden jewelry box that held the pearls my mother gave me on my wedding day, the small diamond studs my grandmother gave me for my sixteenth birthday, my passport, and various oddities— earrings without mates, out-of-fashion earrings, things that needed chains to hang from, chains that needed things to hang on them.

"You know," I told the psychic, "I am in the arts, I do need to move, and I am broke. But I haven't lost any jewelry lately."

Puzzled, he tossed a few more cards on the table, looked down at them and then up at me in surprise.

"Yes, you have," he said. "You lost your wedding ring, figuratively speaking, didn't you? You just got divorced."

"That's right," I said, and glanced at my naked left hand.

"The funny thing is," he continued, "you're not at all upset. In fact, you're glad."

Glad. Not a word one usually associates with a divorce. But that psychic was right; I was glad.

The thesaurus gives joyful, light, lighthearted as synonyms for *glad*. I was all of those things. In the two years before my divorce I had become physically too thin, emotionally too heavy. I felt weighted, like a scuba diver about to drop backward off a boat into the ocean. Sometimes, my chest ached and tightened as if my heart was actually trying to send me a message. I developed insomnia. I stopped cutting my hair. In pictures from that time I am all bones and hair and tight lips. At night, every night, I dreamed I was dead.

As Faith Sullivan writes in *The Cape Ann*, "Being married was like having a hippopotamus sitting on my face, Mrs. Brown. No matter how hard I pushed or which way

I turned, I couldn't get up. I couldn't even breathe. Hippopotamuses aren't all bad. They are what they are. But I wasn't meant to have one sitting on my face." Being unhappily married makes one think that marriage is the hippopotamus, when really it's only one marriage in particular—your own.

On that January afternoon, as I sat in the psychic's apartment on Houston Street in Manhattan, it had only been one week since my husband and I agreed to a divorce. In that week I had grown lighter, lighthearted. One day I found myself walking out of my apartment, onto Hudson Street, and feeling something strange, yet oddly familiar. I had been sleeping well for the first time in years so it wasn't exhaustion. It wasn't hunger; I was eating all of my favorite foods. My work was going well and I had just finished a new novel. I was not yet tired of winter and I was not at all bored. In fact I was ready to leave for three weeks in Egypt. So what was this feeling pressing at my rib cage, demanding to be noticed? I kept walking up Hudson Street, the feeling growing, getting larger, hugging me. A woman passed me and smiled. Suddenly, I recognized what I felt, as if from another lifetime. I was happy.

LAST MONTH my ex-husband called me for advice about his love life.

"What should I do?" he asked me. "You know how I think."

But do I?

I know how he takes his coffee, the type of underwear he prefers. I know when his birthday is and the funny little stories his family tells about him as a child. But after five years together, in many ways he remains an enigma. I am

by
ANN
HOOD

uncertain why we moved from casual friends to dating, from dating to marriage. Why, I have asked myself, did he propose to me? And why did I say yes? Although they say that opposites attract, I have never read that they should marry. And, except for our careers and a love of old movies, there were never two more opposite people. Opposite in temperament, in the ways we live our lives day to day. He was Jewish, hated Manhattan, needed absolute quiet to work; I was Christian, thrived in the city, liked noise. Every summer, I went home to Rhode Island and rented a beach house; he did not like the beach or the noise my Italian relatives who populated the house made.

When reflecting on one's divorce, it is easy to overlook the good things and focus on the reasons why he is an EX-spouse. Certainly my ex-husband was kind and funny and smart and adventurous. On paper, in fact, he was just right. I remember nights back in college when my roommates and I would sit on our bunk beds and make lists of attributes for our perfect man. But how could I know at eighteen, at twenty-one, that there are intangibles that matter more than whether or not someone went to college or how tall they stand?

For years I had lived in an easygoing atmosphere. I had a boyfriend from California who epitomized the term *laid back*. I went to movies alone, enjoying the solitude of a dark theater in the middle of the day. A person who loves to cook, my biggest struggle was with new recipes, my conflicts more of the philosophical variety. Then my ex-husband came into my life and I was introduced to a new way to see the world. He enjoyed disagreeing, over whether to eat Mexican food or Chinese, which movie to rent, or in which museum to spend a Saturday afternoon. It wasn't disagreeing with me that fueled him, it was tension, a charged environment.

I like peace. I like harmony. A friend once told me that when she entertained our small group of friends she knew that everything would go well if I was there. "You have a way of keeping everything nice," she said. Although it is true that my role in my own family is to keep everyone happy, and that there are some people who would argue that all women have that role, I wanted a marriage that ran smoothly. My ex-husband, on the other hand, seemed to enjoy conflict over matters both large and small.

Was it really important to eat burritos instead of fried dumplings? I would ask myself, and forego my craving for margaritas and nachos.

And so on our quiet night together, I scowled over food I didn't really like or want to eat. The marriage wasn't even running smoothly as a result of my giving in all the time. In fact, there was always a new point to debate, a new compromise.

After too many such compromises—not that movie, only science fiction from the midfifties, no museum except the Metropolitan—it did become important where I ate dinner and what movie I watched and which museum I visited. It became so important that a good part of my days was spent negotiating, bickering, angry. Giving up an evening of Mexican food became grounds for war. Then, at night, I would lie in bed wondering what kind of person I had become who fought over eating burritos. When I finally slept, I dreamed, again, that I had died.

———

I BELIEVE in love.

I believe in shaky knees, sweaty palms, a pounding heart.

I believe in love at first sight. I've had it, twice, and they have been my biggest, truest loves.

I believe that being in love, that being loved is, as Elizabeth Cady Stanton said back in 1860, "the open sesame to every soul."

I believe in marriage.

My parents have been married for forty-three years. They still hold hands when they go for a walk. They still kiss each other good night. Their story goes that on the night they met my father asked my mother to marry him. It took three dates for her to say yes. I grew up believing in the power of a love like that. I grew up wanting it. I still do.

I have heard that in Persian the verb "to love" means "to have a friend." Therefore "I love you" means "I have you as a friend." My ex-husband and I began as friends. We drank wine together and played Trivial Pursuit on opposite teams. I liked him. But my knees never shook when he walked in the door. My palms stayed dry. Well, I told myself, passionate, crazy love has gotten you nowhere but brokenhearted. This, I decided, was mature love. It was sensible. We split everything fifty-fifty. The price of a gallon of milk. A tank of gas for a car trip. Household chores.

On my wedding night, I watched a Mets game, then washed the floor of the apartment we were moving out of. He cleaned the bathroom. The wreath of flowers with long ivory ribbons that I thought looked romantic and medieval was tossed into a trash can on Broadway when we went out to get more boxes for packing. Although a part of me was aching that night for some schoolgirl scenario, another part felt grown-up, practical.

In St. Martin, on our honeymoon, he took scuba lessons and I developed claustrophobia. It manifested itself in the hotel swimming pool, when I dropped to the bottom of the deep end wearing weights and a mask. I thought I was suffocating. The thing I loved the most— water—became frightening. I could not go back in without starting to hyperventilate. I sat by the pool, waded in the ocean, but did not swim.

We argued because I thought it would be fun to rent a Jeep and explore the island. "I'll rent anything but a Jeep," he declared. We argued because he would not buy drinks at the poolside bar and instead insisted on walking two-and-a-half blocks to an indoor bar where drinks, though cheaper, could not be taken outside. I sat alone, drinking frozen rum drinks by the pool while he drank inside.

My silk honeymoon chemise was worn once. "Gee," he said, "that makes your legs look weird."

When I called home from St. Martin, I wanted to tell my mother that maybe I had made a mistake. That maybe I was wrong after all, and the less sensible kind of love was the kind I wanted. But I had only been married for three days. So instead I told her how I had won big at the casino, that the weather was great, and that I flunked scuba lessons in the hotel swimming pool. To this day, I am still claustrophobic.

WHEN I was in high school I read an article about love in a women's magazine that advised women to look hard at their new boyfriend's faults rather than at his attributes. Those, the magazine said, would dominate someday. So when friends asked me how come I didn't notice, or care about, the facets of my ex-husband's personality that helped to destroy the marriage, I can only shrug. They were all there from the evening we met. His love for conflict, his need for routine. If you saw them then, someone asked me, why did you get married?

Once I had a roommate who tended toward spells of depression—she wouldn't shower, she overate, she stayed in her robe and watched television all day. I grew to dislike her, to worry every time I walked in the door about what I would find there. When we went our separate ways, we became good friends again. It is so easy to tolerate the quirks and shortcomings of our friends. When my ex-husband and I were friends, I would hang up the phone when he became bellicose, bow out of an evening that didn't include what I wanted to do. I could say that I had a great friend who was a curmudgeon. I could even admire his eccentricities. But when those eccentricities followed me around all day, they were not as endearing.

As writers, we both worked at home, but my ex-husband couldn't work if there was noise—the banging of pans, my laughter on the telephone, the hum of the TV. How could someone who likes music playing in the background, who cooks to cure writer's block, who loves to hear a friend's voice long distance coexist with someone who is bothered by footsteps in the hall outside? When he and I were friends and went away skiing for a weekend, I found it funny to sit in a room with the door closed wearing a headset to watch *Regis and Kathie Lee* so he could work in total quiet. It was a story that my friends and I laughed about. But when it's your life, it isn't as funny.

One of my greatest pleasures is a lazy Sunday morning in bed with the *New York Times,* "All Things Considered," lots of coffee, and the person I love. But my married Sundays were spent alone in bed, my cats on my stomach. "I get too antsy," my ex-husband used to say. If he felt like working on a Sunday morning, he made a no-noise rule. And so, one summer morning, in yet another room alone with the door closed and headphones on, something settled in me. I wanted my life back. I wanted music. I wanted to laugh freely. I wanted to walk through rooms with open doors.

I remembered once being told by someone that he loved me, but wasn't in love with me. Aren't they the same? I had cried. The boy, older, in college, shook his head wisely. Later, I used it myself. I'm sorry, I told someone, I love you, but I'm not in love with you. They're the same thing! he'd insisted. But of course they're not at all the same. I loved my ex-husband. I admired him. I respected him. He made me laugh. But sitting alone that day, I remembered how it felt to be in love. What I was feeling then, what I had always felt, was something different.

Once I decided that, my dreams about being dead stopped. Instead, I dreamed that I lifted from my bed and, with greater and greater speed, began to fly around my apartment. The sensation was wonderful, zooming above my desk, my stove, heading for the window that opened onto the street. Trying to get to that window, I knocked into the brick wall of the living room. The next morning I woke up with bruises on my elbows and knees, convinced I needed to fly away.

For me, the question that most haunts me is not why did you get divorced, but why did you get married? I was thirty, the age when it begins to feel like spinsterdom is around the corner. I was ready to settle down, to make a life with someone. At the start of a new career as a writer, I wanted to plunge into my life, as if all that came before was a warm-up for something more. Somewhere inside me, a voice was screaming: "Let's go!"

But, too, there was the urge to be sensible. After all, I had done nothing in my life to date that was by the book. I had graduated with honors from college and went to work as a flight attendant. I had left everything and everyone I knew behind and moved alone to New York City to become a writer. I had dated men who made me quiver, with passion and longing and love. They were not the men my cousins or friends brought home and married. They were not employed by solid corporations. They did not drive solid automobiles. But I was in love with them. And somehow I always ended up brokenhearted.

Here was a man who fit my qualifications (a writer!) and my family's (a well-published writer!). Even though he didn't have to, he worked nine to five. He was, I thought, a grown-up. And so was I, because I was marrying for companionship and not passion. Soon after my wedding, I began to write a series of short stories about unhappy women who married men for all the wrong reasons and leave them for others with zing. In the early stories, the husbands triumphed, but the more I sat alone in a room with the door closed and earphones on, the more my heroines escaped.

I USED TO harbor some 1970s notion about divorcées. Crowded singles bars. Bad Chablis. Sweaty men wearing too much gold. Women in spandex. There was something sleazy and shameful about it, I thought. But by the time I was ready to do it, that image had faded. I only wanted my old, pre-marriage life back. In many ways, I was uncertain about exactly what that had been. But I remembered how at night I used to sleep well. How being alone felt fine because there was no one down the hall not talking to me, keeping me away. In *The Female Eunuch*, Germaine Greer wrote that "loneliness is never more cruel than when it is felt in close propinquity with someone who has ceased to communicate." That was the loneliness I had begun to feel, the kind that hurt.

Instead of a singles bar of desperate people, I imagined my divorced self happily alone, my music shouting, my phone ringing, eating burritos until I couldn't eat them anymore. I imagined breathing easily again, staying up late, lounging in bed on Sunday mornings. When you live alone, doing these solitary things takes on a different meaning. You are capable, independent, content. But when your husband is in another room, that room's door also closed, those things done alone only make you lonely.

A FRIEND came to visit the other night. She was obviously distraught, puffy-eyed, with the corners of her mouth turned down.

"My husband wants a divorce," she said.

She told me what was going on, how he had changed and they had grown apart. The truth was that a divorce would make her unhappy; she loved him.

But then, past the tears and pain, she whispered, "I don't want to be divorced. To have an ex-husband. A first husband."

And even though I myself was divorced, had an ex-husband, I agreed. "It feels weird," I said.

"But so many people are," my friend said, nodding. "So many are divorced. And they're fine. Why, some have several exes."

"I'm one of those people," I said. "I'm divorced."

I remember my grandmother, disgusted, whispering about someone, "She's divorced."

We were Catholic. Italian. We did not get divorced.

My parents stayed married. So did my friends' parents. My aunts and uncles. What I imagined, what I believed to be true, was that I too would get married and stay that way.

For months before my wedding, I began to have stomach problems. My fiancé went away for a month and I felt happy to be alone. My stomach problems stopped.

"PMJ," a friend told me. "Pre-marital jitters."

But were they? Or was my body trying to talk my mind out of something? I had dinner with an old boyfriend, someone I had loved passionately. My knees still trembled when he walked into the restaurant. I made up games for myself. If this old boyfriend showed up at the wedding like Benjamin did at Elaine's in *The Graduate,* it would be proof that passion wins over logic. If he showed up, I would run off with him while Simon and Garfunkel sang in the background.

My wedding day was beautiful. Clear, not too hot. It was the wedding I had always dreamed of—outdoors, large striped tents, a bevy of bridesmaids in lace. My old love stayed away, my silly fantasy of him playing Benjamin to my Elaine forgotten. I look at those pictures now, study them for clues. There I am, smiling, dancing, head thrown back in laughter. Was I really happy that day? Did I believe the "until death do us part"?

W H E N I got married, I took with me an old oak table and four antique chairs. I had had those chairs for almost ten years. They had survived nine moves, countless parties, the weight of hundreds of people. But when I got married, they began to fall apart. A loose leg, a cracked spindle, a weak seat. Until, one by one, they all broke. For a while, as each one broke, I moved in an old college director's chair to replace it. But then my husband inherited a large dining-room table that dwarfed the director's chairs, and we moved to a bigger apartment, and it seemed like it was time to buy new chairs for the dining room.

Of course, we couldn't agree on what the chairs should be.

Months passed.

We asked neighbors to bring their own chairs when they came for dinner.

For parties, I set up a buffet.

After much arguing, the style was agreed upon at last. We had been, by this time, chairless for over a year.

As I've said, we split everything fifty-fifty. My husband

decided, arbitrarily, that he would spend no more than thirty dollars per chair.

In the past, when he made decisions like that, I simply went out and bought what we needed myself—wineglasses, linen napkins, candlesticks. But this was now at the end of our marriage. Counseling had failed. We both knew it was over. So I didn't go out and buy our chairs. I had invested too much alone already.

I HAVE SEEN the pain of divorce.

Custody battles. Bad financial settlements. Children caught in the middle, taken away, turned against a parent.

I cannot say what other people should do. I cannot say that divorce is good. I cannot say that it is right.

I can only say that my divorce saved me. I weigh ten pounds more and feel hundreds of pounds lighter.

For me, the divorce was not difficult. I had been living in loneliness for years by the time my marriage ended, so that being alone felt uplifting, free. Still, I do not want to get divorced again, though I want to re-marry. Instead, I want to get married right this time—for love and passion and shaky knees. And I want it to last.

LAST WEEK my ex-husband called me for advice about an apartment he was considering.

"The street is noisy," he said. "It gets heavy truck traffic."

"Forget about it," I told him.

"It'll drive me crazy when I'm working, right?" he said.

"You couldn't even stand the sound of laughter," I reminded him.

It wasn't until later that I thought about how, over our years together, he heard less and less laughter from me. At the end, there was none at all. I had robbed him, too, with my unhappiness, my bad moods, my frustration.

I laugh a lot these days.

When a friend commented that it was weird how my ex-husband and I called each other for advice, I laughed about his funny quirks, how the sound of trucks would send him straight to Bellevue. It struck me as endearing, his need for absolute quiet. Back before we were husband and wife, I found that lovable; I find it so again now.

"But you're divorced," this friend reminded me. "You're not supposed to be such good friends."

But that is just what we are. Good friends. Since our divorce, he has shared holidays with my family, played with my new baby, had drinks with my boyfriend. He has moved into Manhattan, the city he refused to live in when we were married, the city I love. He rents a beach house now with friends. For some reason, these things do not bother me. He has found other sources for conflict, I suppose, and I have found my old life, my old self again. Apart, we are happy. Apart, we can say "I love you" as the Persians meant it—"I have you as a friend." It's a wonderful divorce.

AN
HISTORICAL
ROMANCE

BY *Susan Spano*

I AM a very lucky woman. I have never been caught in the middle of a bloody revolution, gone hungry, suffered serious illness, or seen someone I love die. They say the loss of one's child is the worst, which may partly explain why I remain childless, and in general travel light through life. I fear loss, and have probably impoverished myself by avoiding possessions that could be snatched away. The worst thing that ever happened to me was my divorce, which took away my marriage, and something I loved even more—my husband.

"My life closed twice before it closed," Emily Dickinson wrote, despite the fact that she lived an apparently ruffleless life, filled with flowers, recipes, and letters from loved ones. No one knows exactly what happened to her on those two occasions, but if her father only scolded her or her kitten ran away, what does it matter? She knew loss, because she described it perfectly—and I've known it too.

Still, oddly, I do not regret putting on the drop-waisted, pearl-colored gown my mother wore when she married my father just after World War II and making my own vows one overcast spring morning in a small Protestant church on Cape Cod some forty years later. Nor do I even regret loving the man with whom I made those vows. We stayed married for six years, and it's been four since we divorced. Four springs have come and gone with their lilac mementos of my wedding, and Easter Sundays to remind me of the desperate time when things flew apart. What I do regret now is the way I loved him—beyond measure and reason, through a romantic veil that I have only now begun to part.

Don't get me wrong. When I fell in love (such an interesting phrase—did I lose my footing or get pushed from some higher, firmer place?) I was not a green girl, eager to put my quirky mind, pining body, and excellent liberal education to use as some man's perfect mate. I came up after the feminist revolution among sophisticated people; my mother worked all through her married life and would have made a bang-up career woman had three children not come along. She and my father wanted most of all that I should get ahead, do well, achieve. And I was a good daughter, so I tried hard.

You see how lucky I was? No one stopped me from reading the Brontës, Austen, and Tolstoy at just about the time I got a training bra, mascara, and black patent leather heels for my confirmation. No one knew what a hash I'd make of novels like *Pride and Prejudice,* how I'd come to view even dashed, hopeless love as beautiful and fail to discriminate between Emma Bovary and the heroines of the historical romances I also devoured, sitting in the deep wing chair in my parents' bedroom with a stack of graham crackers by my side. They of the deep cleavages and life-transforming loves. In college I learned how the great heroines diverged from the paperback ones, but it was too late; I knew that love was complicated, self-referential, not the be-all and end-all, but I felt something different. I was like a crisp-looking chocolate with a soft fruity heart.

Now I have a dear friend with a daughter that tender, poignant age who reads the same books I read, leading me to worry. Of course, I do not blame all my romantic turmoils on the syllabus of my youth, and would not ban the great books I misconstrued from households where young women live. In fact, a certain eroticism that can enrich a girl's life rises from a simple-minded reading of the "greats," whispering of the strange, wild realm of sex in the desert of fumbling adolescence. And my friend's daughter—who, after attending my wedding, asked her parents for a bride doll—was old enough to know that something had gone very wrong with my picture-perfect marriage when my husband stopped appearing at my side. Doubtless in this day and age, she also has friends with divorced parents and has glimpsed the limitations of love. So maybe she already understands the decidedly unromantic lessons of *Madame Bovary.* Maybe she's even harboring a tough, useful little kernel of cynicism deep inside. Maybe all childen who have felt at first hand or observed divorce will grow up a little more levelheaded about love than I was.

Certainly divorce can have disastrous effects on children, and I count myself lucky again to have parents still married after fifty years. But would a kiss from Mr. Rochester have seemed quite so earth-moving had I suspected that romance is a pattern woven in lies? What else—besides his goldenness—would I have noticed when, as a college sophomore, I saw for the first time the boy who became my husband? For, of course, I loved him at first sight.

by
SUSAN
SPANO

NOW YOU KNOW me, at least as well as I know myself—and certainly better than I knew myself when I was my husband's wife, living on a tree-lined street of brownstones in a dicey part of Brooklyn. Around the corner was a restaurant run by Panamanians where we drank *café con leche*, a fish store where the mussels were occasionally off, and a Laundromat where I did our clothes even when it was really his turn. That I managed more than my fair share of the housework didn't bother me though; I was more fastidious, and he was so busy—an actor of considerable accomplishments, even if most of his starring roles were out of town. Nor did I mind our frequent, long separations because I loved his career in the theater, had my own writing and editing work to do, was by nature a solitary soul, and got to visit him for opening nights in interesting places, always wearing fancy new clothes. When he returned after a show had closed, we were tentative, relearning first how to cook together, then how to talk and be together, as well. The old sexual heat between us had cooled—I assumed that's what happened in marriage—replaced with an intense physical sweetness, and he was always telling me he loved me.

At least, that's how I remember it. He was usually cast as a romantic leading man, and was adept at the role; but in real life he was my very own tall blond lead—I never doubted that. I'm now shocked by how willing to make sacrifices I was (perhaps because female self-sacrifice somehow seemed a necessary adjunct to romantic love), and think that our sex life was a kind of penury. But I can also recall lying in bed with him in the late afternoon, touching his brow, imagining that rays glinted from it, as if from some rare, burnished coin. I should be embarrassed to tell it, but I'm not. Maybe to regret you must love like that, I don't know. Maybe I simply still don't want to let that dreaming girl in her parents' wing chair go.

ONE RAINY March day just after he'd returned from the road, he was in the bedroom lifting weights and preparing for a difficult audition.

I was in the kitchen foraging for lunch.

He came to me and announced that he wasn't going to the audition, which amazed me though I didn't press him for a reason, just let him slip back into the bedroom to think. I stood there while the canned tomato soup bubbled on the stove, realizing something was happening—something big and bad, but I didn't know what. Then, as if directed by a voice outside myself, I followed him, stopping at the edge of the bed where he sat, his shoulders slumped, head down, and asked ever-so-slightly playfully, "Is another shoe going to drop?" But he said nothing, so I left.

He did not reappear for an hour, though I knew he'd used the phone. At last he came into the living room, standing before me this time, and said, "I've been seeing other women."

That is how my life once closed, though it went ach-ingly slow; I pushed hard against the shutting door and he couldn't clear himself away from it so easily either. I'm not sure what he was feeling, though I spent far too much energy trying to figure it out, to my own detriment. Now I've claimed this story as my own; I am its protagonist. I live with myself now, not him. I take care of myself—from my own laundry to my soul.

But I did not take care of myself then. I turned my face directly to the ugliness beneath the calm surface of our lives, sifting through it relentlessly, demanding facts in or-der to correctly reinterpret the past I'd lived through so ignorantly. He provided them like a shamed schoolboy pulling stolen marbles out of his pocket. I learned in a series of lacerating quizzes that he'd had affairs with many of the actresses in his plays, though he'd tidily ended the relationships before coming home; he'd loved just one of them four years ago and might have told me so had she felt the same way about him; I knew them all, because he'd introduced us, even sought my opinion of their acting skills (as if they had to meet my high standards before he'd take them to bed); he used to call me early every night, so that I wouldn't call him later and wonder where he was. During that awful time, I'd wake every morning at three with another question lying beside my head on the pil-low—nightmare monsters that wanted to be fed; some-times I wake to them still.

Betrayal was something completely new to me. It took its power from the fact that the person I loved most had found the worst way to hurt me. "At least I told you," he once said—he was staying temporarily with a male friend and we'd met at a restaurant in the Village (a safe zone) to

139

by

SUSAN
SPANO

talk. *Yes*, I thought, *you are like an abuser who feels better for taking his wife to the emergency ward after beating her up.* I saw what he'd done as abuse for a time, and even attended a meeting for the "co-dependent spouses of alcoholics," since there were no groups for the co-dependent spouses of cheaters. Like some tired old cliché, I riffled through his desk drawers when he was away, checking his old calendars for salient dates and amassing phone numbers, fantasizing about divorce-court dramas and surprise phone calls to his lovers. *Hi, just wanted to tell you I know. Ever hear of sisterhood, you bitch?* And I once even incited him to threaten violence. We'd just come from another futile couples therapy session during which I'd listened to him try to articulate his confusion: He didn't know why he'd slept around, whether we should split up, if he loved me—indeed, what love was. I was very close to ending it and had already met with a lawyer; but I wanted more clarity before I made the decision to divorce, and to be a full player in the drama, if or when the final curtain dropped.

We were on the steep flight of steps that led up to our apartment when I accused him of lying about the latest in his string of women, who clearly loved him since she'd urged him to tell me the truth. And he'd told me, which had to mean that he loved her too, wanted to be with her, not me. Why couldn't he just say so and let me off the hook, show enough courage to be cruel but kind? I stumbled; he reached out to steady me and I knocked him away; he pushed me into the living room, with an arm raised.

"I'm not lying anymore. I *don't* love her," he said.

"Go ahead and hit me," I replied.

And then he started to cry.

I'd forgotten this until just now. I don't know what it means—that he either loved me in his way or didn't love me at all.

Between such episodes, when we both aired ugly parts of ourselves we never knew we had, I spent most of my time loathing myself. My friends queried me gently: *Weren't you a little suspicious? He was an actor, after all. Are you sure you didn't know? How was the sex between you?* (All I can say—then and now—is that I didn't know, and that the sex seemed good enough for me). So, on top of the betrayal, I got to feel ashamed. I got to hate myself, when the rage of Medea would have served me better; but I was ever a stranger to rage.

Easter was coming on during the worst of it, when people in the most wonderful hats lined up outside evangelical churches in Brooklyn storefronts with neon crosses. The cherry blossoms in the Botanical Garden were in bud, and I took to running for hours and miles, pounding out my pain in a season too beautiful for words, a place too ugly and lovely all at once. In the midst of everything I must admit a certain joy and frisson of excitement. *Great people can change their lives at will,* I thought. *I'm not great, but I can let change come, try to embrace it. What will happen to me? What will I become?*

My family and friends and all the green of spring sympathized with me, but my favorite stroke came from a woman on the street in Brooklyn, with three children in tow. I was running and crying at the same time, and when I passed her she called out, "It's a man. You cryin' cuz of a man." I slowed until she drew a Bible out of her bag, then ran on.

I DID NOT find what I needed in therapy, although I tried dutifully. I could talk until the cows came home, articulating things that were true, for the moment at least. My husband could not talk at all. So there was no real communication. Our brief stint in couples therapy was a stop-gap measure, a way of asserting: *We are trying to work this out.* But I wonder. Possibly he just wanted to be rid of me as compassionately as he knew how, by putting me in the hands of a professional caregiver. I should have heard him when he said that he did not know if he loved me. It's just that he'd said he loved me so many times before. The dark had come so suddenly. I could still close my eyes and imagine day.

So, in an assertively cheerful office with Kleenex boxes strategically placed, we embarked upon what we took to calling "the process," leading where I did not know. But if we cut away the tangled emotional undergrowth, it seemed to me faintly possible that a better, new marriage awaited us; he would have to understand what he had done to me and why, then ask for forgiveness in a deeply felt way; I would have to see if I could forgive him. I started reading self-help books and thinking about psychology for the first time, which led me to a new vision of marriage as a beautiful, intricate machine—like an heirloom ormolu clock—that must be constantly worked on to keep it going, with the help of a therapist. I did not particularly like the idea of admitting a paid third party into our marriage for the long haul, but the allure of the reconceived marriage was strong; it seemed a worthy substitute for romantic love, which had so let me down. At any rate, I was willing to try.

Of course, part of "the process" required that we both ask why our marriage had gone wrong, or more precisely, what each of us had done that had allowed my husband to take lovers. I approached the question with typical earnestness and self-involvement—for I tended always to turn it back on myself: *What had I done wrong? Had I in some way encouraged him to play around?* Friends noticed this tendency, and perceived it as unhealthy self-blame; given the situation, it seemed obvious to them that my husband was the miscreant, not me. Even my father—my family's Buddha—advised me to forget "the process." "Whatever the hell that is," he said. "Cut him loose right away."

But I knew a few things my father and friends didn't, or at least suspected things I only figured out later. My husband loved me—or once had—else why all the anguish? We'd *both* undervalued the importance of sex in marriage by letting it change and then languish; we should have worked to make it remain a central part of our lives, and he shouldn't have solved the problem in his own way. My penchant for being alone—which has turned out to be a great treasure to me now—had permitted him to seek the society of others. And surely most significant, by casting him in the role of the romantic leading man who'd brought me into his golden aureole by marrying me, I'd failed to see who he really was, weaknesses and all. Frankly, I'd failed to see anything beside myself and my own crippling romantic dream.

These are all good things to know, but I learned them by myself, without the help of a therapist. During sessions with her, she returned constantly to one question: *Why did he tell you about the affair now?* I realized what she was driving at, of course—that he'd done so now because he wanted out. But I couldn't reach that conclusion yet. When I even let myself contemplate it I grew angry at last. He'd told me the truth and sworn never to lie again— great. He was engaged in "the process"—swell. But if what he already knew or was finding out therein was that he wanted a divorce, then he had to say so; I wanted to hear the words from him.

WOMEN are more emotional than men. I hate to generalize, but in my experience this has proven so often the case that I take it for an axiom. What is more, being emotional fills a particular need in many women, filled by many men in a different way. Men do—they play sports, prefer seeing a movie to talking, trek in Patagonia, or at least imagine such adventures; women talk, ruminate, feel. But for me, feeling is itself an adventure, a journey through fearful, turmoiled places, an odyssey or hegira. Along the feeling way, there are tight, dangerous passages where one must decide whether to take a side path down into the valley or carry on. Feeling as far into a crisis as one can requires, like adventure, equal measures of courage and stupidity. I am happy and healthy enough now to be able to look back at the endgame of my marriage with a mixture of pride and amusement. How far along the feeling way I went. However, I would not want to undertake that particular emotional adventure again.

After a month of intensive therapy, my husband rejoined the cast of the play he'd been acting in before he told me about his affairs, though this time the production was booked at a theater in California, a continent away. I could have challenged him not to go, but didn't want my marriage to hang on this particular, relatively mundane issue; he could have given up the play, but wasn't compelled to—a sign I couldn't read at the time, even if it now seems as electric as any in Times Square. Then too, the distance might help, I thought, though the fact that his most recent lover was also in the cast certainly would not. Still, he swore he'd broken off with her and didn't intend to recommence the affair.

She felt differently, and pursued him—on the apparent assumption that it was now morally permissible to do so. But he held fast, even reading me the notes she wrote to him; everything between us was to be open and honest now, so we could see what was left of our relationship. We had marathon telephone conversations full of tears and recriminations, babble and stony silence, kind and hard words. His former lover occasionally tempted him, he admitted, but was chiefly an irritation. He was fully in "the process" now, in a way he hadn't been before.

The truth is that he was in his "process" and I was in mine, the two bound to intersect only one more time. Meanwhile, back in Brooklyn, I was also coming to life; frozen for so many years, the "soul's sap quivered," to paraphrase T. S. Eliot. Doubtless, the poet could not have anticipated that someday his words would be taken to include a newborn interest in sexy lingerie, maniacal exercise, exploratory forays into singles bars, and the relentless search for willing listeners to tell my story to. I confessed the ugly truth to almost everyone I knew, and even made new friends so that I could tell them too. Revenge partly motivated me, since bruiting my husband's sins seemed a reasonable if inadequate way of getting back at him. But I also experienced the satisfaction of letting others into my life (formerly my husband's sole domain), and of their reciprocation—which came, I'm sure, simply because I'd at last dared to show them how far from perfect my life was. These friends—most of them female, because women make such good friends—are with me now, at the other end of the phone whenever I need them, as they were then.

One day several weeks after he'd left town, my husband had a fantasy that he shared with me about the two of us living in a woodframe cottage in Vermont, with cross-country skis leaning in the corner, spicy smells emanating from the kitchen, a dog by the hearth, and a baby in a highchair. He was very confused. Nonetheless, the vision had a staggering effect on me; I could take or leave Vermont, but the baby clinched it. Of course, I failed to recognize this as simply the postscript to a historical romance, the happily-ever-aftering of a leading lady and man. The moment seemed ripe to get together again, so I bought a ticket to California.

Later I decided that the airlines played a significant part in the termination of my marriage. If I'd sprung for the nine-hundred-dollar ticket that would have gotten me to California immediately, maybe we'd have caught the wave of my husband's feeling. Instead, while I waited for two weeks to leave in order to fly on the cheap, the wave broke.

Of course, I didn't know that when I finally arrived, sidewinded by the balminess and palm trees. I only knew that the reunion wasn't one of the most heightened moments of my life. At the airport we hugged like two logs that had fallen on each other in the forest. He looked strange to me, and not entirely attractive, with his hair oddly combed. But gradually it fell back into its accustomed blond disarray, and I started to know him again. He was the man I'd loved for more than a decade, beginning before he had hair on his chest. He *was* love to me. Never an abstract. Always him.

We argued again when we arrived at the apartment where he was staying, about I can't remember what and it doesn't matter—except that in so doing we fell back into the roles of wronged wife and shamed-but-angry-errant husband. Then he told me about a book he'd just found at a secondhand shop in the neighborhood. Now this strikes me as a ridiculous California cliché—next stop EST, then transcendence. But I was so achingly vulnerable that I listened.

"I recognize myself in it," he said. "It's about becoming a fully sexual being." He smiled sheepishly. "It's called *The Way of the Lover*. Here, I'll read you some of it."

We were sitting at opposite ends of a couch. I felt at once jet-lagged and adrenaline-charged. He began reading a passage about bad relationships, couples who stay together out of fear or guilt. Though tears started dribbling out of my eyes, he ignored them, perhaps because he'd seen me cry so many times before. But on some level I noted his unresponsiveness and filed it away. It was a new development.

It was *the* development. I stayed for two more days, slowly realizing that he wasn't even acting as if he loved me anymore. While there, I cheered at the film *Thelma and Louise*, considered the overtures of a handsome bicyclist I met in a park, saw my husband's play, if only to count the ways the actress who had been his lover was beggared in comparison to me, and felt the sun on my breasts at a nude beach north of town. I suppose, it was my turn to be a California cliché.

The end came with no fanfare, over dinner in a Mexican restaurant. He had a few days off, and the keys to a friend's condo in the mountains. But why he was contemplating taking me there I did not know; I could feel nothing from him; he had finally stopped lying—even on a thespic level.

And so I calmly said (again as if directed by some voice outside myself), "This isn't really working, is it? Don't you think I should go home and file for divorce?"

He cried and wanted to know how I could be so strong. He had no idea how strong I was, though I was beginning to see the full extent of his weakness. I'd been his victim, yet was also forced to be our judge. For some time I thought making me say the words was the worst, most immoral thing he'd done. But he didn't make me say them; I know that now. I'd reached the decision myself, in my own harrowing way.

BUT THERE *is* a moral point here. I hesitate to even suggest it, remembering how the eyes of many of my wise, loving friends glaze over at the very mention of *morality*. *Adultery* has much the same effect. But bear with me, postmoralist thinkers, as I cut to the chase and finally consider the question of right and wrong. For, you see, I tried to work this out through psychology, which helped, but only so far.

For a time, I simply thought that breaking one's marriage vows was wrong, but then therapy helped me realize that marriage has always been and must still be elastic, that it can be refined and even fortified by troubles. Beyond that, I knew something about infidelity myself, having once cheated on a boyfriend. So I was not lily white.

Later, my dear friend with the teenage daughter put a new spin on things for me, though. She loved my husband, partly because simply by marrying him I had told her that she should. And when he betrayed me she wrote him a letter, because she felt betrayed too. In it she said: "It is a fundamental and absolute violence to willfully withhold from anyone the information she would need to make clear and rational choices about the substance and direction of her life. I am so thrown myself when I think of you—how can there suddenly be no you as I thought I knew and valued you—that I can't begin to imagine what it must be like inside Susan's head sometimes."

For a while I rested there, thinking that it is simply immoral to lie—and so hanged my husband. But I have moved on, and am likely to again, incessantly beating back. Now I can understand how my husband got drawn into a lie he was too weak to contain. I don't, however, believe that he didn't know he was hurting me—indeed, I even think he was occasionally blithe about it. This strikes me now as the true heart of the matter. Now I believe that it is immoral to be cruel. No matter how weak you are, willful cruelty is immoral. There are no excuses. Everyone must, to that extent, be strong.

I SAW MY HUSBAND just two more times after that—once to divide the contents of our apartment and again entirely by chance. I did go back to Brooklyn, file for divorce, and flee, living for a year in the country, because a farmhouse in the northwest corner of Connecticut was offered to me. Can you imagine such luck? Such good friends?

If you have never been in New England in the summer, you cannot know what a Gilead it is, what true therapy there is in long walks beside the Housatonic River with an old dog, a telephone, books of poetry, peonies beside the fence, beets from the garden, and scotch on the rocks. Scotch is a New England thing—regardless, it was a drug I needed.

I convalesced slowly, time after time resisting the urge to call my soon-to-be ex-husband (generally when I'd had one more nip than was truly therapeutic). Before we'd parted, he told me that one of the reasons he hadn't been able to make the decision to divorce was his fear that he'd never see me again, that I would blot him out of my life. This, after all, is what I told him I would do, partly to punish him, and partly because I knew that friendship between us was impossible. I didn't care for him as a friend, I loved him. Now I had to stop loving him; seeing him would only make that harder. I knew many divorced couples who'd actually divorced in a friendly manner or become friends after splitting up; that they could do so amazed me, and seemed a mark of wisdom and maturity.

Maybe, someday, I could be that wise and mature, I thought. But I doubted it, because in my utter withdrawal from my ex-husband something else was going on. I'd thereby given the divorce meaning, made it one of my touchstones.

Toward the end of that first summer I went into Manhattan for the day. Since filing for divorce, I'd taken to tinting my hair and had found a stylist near my ex-therapist's office. I was on the subway heading there, sitting with my nose in a book. The Number One train stopped at Seventy-second Street and the doors opened, then closed. For several minutes nothing happened, so I looked up to see what was wrong.

He was sitting directly across from me, watching me. I felt my face turn red. The doors opened and closed again, as they sometimes do. I stood up.

And I suppose because he didn't know what else to do, he giggled nervously. I could have spat blood at him and damned fate for putting him on that train at that particular moment—I don't know which I hated more.

The doors opened once again. I walked off before they reclosed and the train finally clattered on.

MY FRIENDS look at my life since the end of my marriage and say I've got to be careful, because I'm going to have a hard time opening up to a man, if and when the right one comes along. Perhaps they're right. Perhaps I'm far from healed. I do sometimes still see a tall blond in the street and think briefly that it's my ex-husband. I do sometimes say vile things about him. And I do still have a hard time in the spring.

But I am surer now than ever before that I walked the right road toward my divorce, and that I have nearly let the love I felt for my ex-husband go. However, I don't want to see him again—ever. This is the stamp I put on my divorce, the meaning. I'm no longer afraid that I'd fall for him again if I did (believe me, what I felt on the subway wasn't love). I just don't want him to look into my face and giggle. I want my absence from his life to stand for something—that he was weak and cruel once, and that it was wrong.

By the same token, I don't want to let myself forget that I romanticized him, and in so doing made any true marriage between us impossible. I will always be drawn to romantic love but have learned that outside paperback novels, it's corrosive. Part sex, part makeup and lights, part need. Something to be wary of, to get beyond. In another year or so, I'm going to give my friend's daughter Virginia Woolf and hope that *A Room of One's Own* can still have meaning in her post-feminist world—as it must, for a sexist society cannot be transformed until women's hearts are.

These I take to be the lessons of my divorce, not of my marriage. I wonder if I ever really was married in the truest sense, and now take the much-adjusted ormolu clock model of matrimony to be the best. It is given to some couples to learn and grow in wedlock. "The faults of married people continually spur up each of them, hour by hour, to do better and to meet and love upon a higher ground," Robert Louis Stevenson wrote.

It was given to me to learn and grow in divorce.

A FAILED DIVORCE

BY *Alix Kates Shulman*

*W*HY ARE terminated marriages called "failed," as
though endurance were all? Perhaps a marriage, however
brief, ought to be counted a success if it achieves the pur-
pose for which it was undertaken—whether sexual
heaven, freedom from parental rule, financial benefit, le-
gitimization of children, companionship, citizenship. By
this measure, some of the most successful marriages I
know (including my first one) have been short. Of course,
a marriage can also bring unexpected dire consequences:
miserable sex, bondage, financial dependence or ruin,
wretched children, boredom, terror. Such outcomes, to
my mind, would damn a marriage as failed even (or particularly) if it should last unto death.

Similarly, a divorce can accomplish various ends and
perhaps ought also to be counted a failure or success in
light of the consequences. So a divorce that redeemed a

decent marriage before it failed or gave a proper burial to a putrefying one might be regarded as successful, while one that tormented the parties long after the final papers were signed might well be deemed a failure. Of my own two divorces, one was successful, one failed. The successful one was short, snappy, and to the point; the other one was drawn out, bitter, and messy—in these respects resembling the marriages they ended.

WHAT I EXPECTED

In the world of suburban Cleveland, Ohio, where I grew up in the 1930s and 1940s, any marriage that lasted less than forever was judged a failure and any divorce a disgrace. Divorce was so unacceptable that my friend Lydia announced that her father had died at Pearl Harbor rather than admit (as my mother later told me) that her parents had been divorced. In contrast, when the father of Cecily, another classmate, really did die (of heart failure), his daughter easily, if tearfully, acknowledged the truth. Not so Harriet, who moved from New York to Cleveland in junior high with her divorced mother. Sophisticated, and attractive enough to model for a local department store, Harriet's mother was presumed to be turning tricks whenever she had a date, a charge that rubbed off on innocent Harriet to ruin her social life. Where I grew up, divorced plus pretty equaled slut.

No doubt Harriet's mother had another view. In the larger world, where there were more possibilities than vamp or victim, it wasn't divorce per se that mattered, but who left whom and with how many children. In Hollywood movies of the time, divorcées were as often gay, glamorous, and independent as they were pathetic, pitiful, and defeated. Rita Hayworth, Liz Taylor, Eddie Cantor, and Artie Shaw were renowned for the number of times they married and divorced—and proud of it. On the other hand, in books, abandoned women sometimes killed themselves.

The incidence of divorce in the United States which, like that of marriage, had been gradually increasing since the turn of the century, blipped upward abruptly just after World War II: all those forty-eight-hour-pass romances with uniformed heroes that couldn't survive the disappointment of civvies; the fatal strain of separation; international hanky-panky. (This, despite the fact that in most states, to obtain a divorce you had to prove adultery, abandonment, or some sordid crime—unless you took off half a year of your life to establish residence in Reno, or flew to another country if you could afford it.) But whatever the statistics, in white middle-class Cleveland Heights, divorce remained a scandal. The only thing worse, we believed, was never to marry at all—like "Aunt" Esther, the sister-in-law of my uncle Harry, a sad, skinny Gal Friday with her hair in a bun who sat quietly at our family gatherings, as embarrassing as a sixth finger. So much worse, in fact, that years later a friend confessed to me that she'd invented a husband for herself and kept in her wallet a false chronology of her life that could accommodate a husband and a divorce. Divorce was a clear admission of failure, but not to marry was catastrophe.

I shared these views but also had glimmerings of others. My mother, who in the 1930s worked as a designer of history projects for the WPA, had several divorced friends, all more interesting than the married moms. While squarely centered in the striving suburban middle class, my mother became involved through her work with Cleveland's bohemian set: artists, intellectuals, musicians, and dancers who divorced as unselfconsciously as they undressed. Of her two best friends (in turn, mothers of two of my best friends, until third grade), one, a modern dancer whose artist husband died young, kept on marrying and divorcing and remarrying until she reached her fifth husband, and the other, a fellow historian at the WPA and wife of a celebrated violinist, divorced her husband when their daughter was eight and moved to the capital where, in the wartime boom, she developed a successful import-export business and remained confidently single. My mother's boss, a deep-voiced woman named Mary ("Lefty") Warner, with a powerful stride, broad smile, cropped brown hair she wore slicked straight back in a ducktail, and the kindest eyes I've ever seen, shared a house with her vivacious long-haired lover, Andrea Garrison, and Andrea's two teenage children, Danny and Ellen, all handsome, rangy redheads. That Andrea and Lefty were lovers seemed less remarkable to me than that Andrea was divorced, rendering her children pitifully fatherless. The spirited parties at their house, where my parents were the token straights, were—and remain—high points of my childhood: Andrea in flowing chiffon, Lefty in tailored slacks and shirt; animated debates, witty chatter, music, forbidden jokes, booze. Except for my four doting aunts, Lefty was quite my favorite grown-up. I am still grateful for her flattering attentions to me, as if I were an adult, and her patient expectation that I learn to strip all the way down to the white bone the delicious spare ribs she barbecued to a perfect crisp in their fireplace. But the

Garrisons, despite their flaming hair, are to this day a cipher to me. I cannot recall them without the embarrassment I always felt seeing Danny and Ellen fatherless, stripped of their birthright by divorce. That was the image that remained after my mother left her job and they vanished from our lives.

WHAT I SAW

Happily, my parents were as permanently coupled as a pair of gulls. (They are still married, at eighty-seven and ninety-three.) Alone of seven siblings (five sisters, two brothers), my mother maintained a neat nuclear family all her life, though not quite as neat as it appeared: When her brother's wife died in childbirth, my parents adopted the baby and promptly created me, so that a brother eleven months my senior was waiting to greet me when I arrived. In the early years, his father (my uncle), who lived in Pennsylvania and whom we called Papadear, paid us annual visits—until he remarried and stopped coming. One of my mother's sisters ran off to Chicago to live with a married man; one was falsely accused of murdering her husband who blew out his brains; one left her husband behind to travel solo around the world on a tramp steamer; and one, local radio's "Singing Lady," also died in childbirth, giving me a second brother for a few years, until his father remarried and took him back. I remember the wrenching day my uncle came to take away my baby brother, still see the once jolly, plump six-year-old stretch out his dimpled arms and wail for my mother, who stood weeping beside me until long after the black coupe had disappeared over Bradford Hill. From that day on I knew the suffering of orphans, the havoc of a broken family, whether by death or divorce, which as far as I could see came to much the same thing. Soon my little brother became just another cousin, thin and sad. Of all seven siblings in my mother's family, only three had children and only one, my mother, was actually able to raise them. Still, as a child in love with both my parents, I unquestioningly assumed the inevitability, superiority, and necessity of the nuclear family. The families of both my parents were touched repeatedly by death and devastation—but never by divorce, which in some ways seemed worse, because unknown.

And yet, when I left Cleveland for New York at twenty, part of what I fled was that neat, predictable suburban sentence of coupledom, by which one's life seemed permanently settled at twenty-two. Having enjoyed in college a secret affair with a married professor my father's age, a father of five, I was already somewhat cynical about marriage. Not that I would eschew it myself—this was 1953, after all, and I was a woman. But with such counterexamples before me as my mother's glamorous friends and my wayward aunts, I determined to marry only on my own terms. Which meant that divorce, however unacceptable to the children of Cleveland Heights, must be my secret failsafe, my emergency exit. As necessary to a decent life as the possibility of abortion.

(Recently, I discovered in my parents' attic a folder of my freshman themes, from forty years ago. One is on the Salem witch trials; another, entitled "The Great Illusion," presents the following thesis: "Because of our modern American way of life, mate selection must result from intelligent analysis, rather than from romantic love, if successful marriages are to ensue." Evidently, as a college freshman I was already leery of the consequences of losing one's heart, already practical about marriage.)

WHAT I DID

In New York, resenting the confines of dorm life (back when all dorms were single-sex, and curfews for women were strictly enforced), I married a fellow grad student before a year was out. I married partly for the privileges of adulthood, which meant freedom from external control, both parental and *in loco parentis,* partly for the fun of it, and partly to get the damned thing over with. Certainly not in order to settle down. Though I changed my name to my husband's and took a job to support us, it felt less like marriage than going steady—plus cohabitation and sanctioned sex. No wonder that five years later, at the age of twenty-five, I took five days of vacation time to fly to Ciudad Juárez, Mexico, and file papers for the first divorce in my family. When I untied the satin ribbon to read the document, the grounds, printed with a flourish on the crisp parchment paper, were specified as *"incompat-ible de temperamento"*—incompatibility of temperament, which, considering that the only grounds for divorce in New York was adultery, sounded rather frivolous. However, to my father, an upright lawyer, it was important that I avoid the scandal of a New York divorce (even though by then I had already begun to live with my next husband, who was awaiting *his* first divorce), and I was happy to oblige: I'd never been to Mexico.

That divorce seemed to me little more than a useful piece of paper, like the marriage that had led to it:

practical, even necessary, but slightly absurd. (Why should a paper determine one's living arrangements?) Once it was final, I never saw my ex-husband again, nor did we speak until, on the eve of his second marriage, he phoned to ask if I'd be willing to submit to an Orthodox Jewish divorce to satisfy his new wife's family. Apparently each jurisdiction required its own particular form of hocus-pocus; but whether the magic words appeared in English, Spanish, or Aramaic, sanctified by a judge, *abogado,* or *rebbe* made no difference to me, as long as they left me free. Again, I gladly obliged.

SURPRISE

My second marriage, to a man who became the father of my children, was another matter entirely. This was far more serious than going steady. Although I entered into it in the same carefree spirit as I had my first, dashing down to City Hall on my lunch hour and returning to work in the afternoon, once I quit my job to have children, nothing else about this marriage was remotely like the other. Living in a Manhattan apartment beyond my means with two babies, no income, and a philandering husband, I suddenly found myself as vulnerable and dependent as any traditional suburban housewife. No longer could I think of marriage as a lark, a pleasure, or a convenience; now it was the structure and lifeline of my children's lives. The debate about marriage has long been confounded by the fact that for some marriage is a prison and divorce a relief, while for others, particularly women with young children, marriage is a protection and divorce (given the virtual impossibility of enforcing child support) an impoverishment; and although the various reforms of marriage laws throughout this century have frequently operated to privilege the married, the institution has had such a complex history that what feels oppressive to one woman feels like security to another, depending not only on the class, occupation, and relative power of the people involved but on their personal relations, ambitions, and feelings. Once I had children, divorce, which I had always held in reserve to bail me out, turned from failsafe to threat; if my marriage came to an end, my children could be left fatherless, penniless, and bereft, fulfilling the worst anxieties of my childhood. The mother of my school friend Harriet suddenly flashed before me, a perilous shooting star.

When I realized the seriousness of my situation, I scrambled to alleviate my dependence and strengthen my position. I searched for freelance work I could do at home, took a sweet lover of my own, and, discovering a newly reborn feminism, embraced the movement that, with its dazzling ideas and expanding numbers, enabled me both to understand and to fight my predicament.

This is not the place to detail the profound influence of feminist ideas on my perception of marriage, motherhood, and divorce—ideas that transformed me from an anxious, homebound observer into an active shaper of my own life. But as part of my transformation, a decade into my second marriage, I drew up a marriage agreement by which my husband and I committed ourselves to equal responsibility for child care and housework. In 1969 when I wrote the agreement, the idea of equality in marriage was so outrageous that the piece appeared in many magazines including *New York*, *Ms.*, *Redbook*, and *Life*, which gave it a six-page spread, and was attacked by Norman

Mailer, S. I. Hayakawa, and Russell Baker, among others. But, like the world that rests on the back of a turtle, at bottom, our agreement, for all the hoopla surrounding it, rested on nothing more substantial than our own floating goodwill. When that failed, we separated.

THE TRIAL

Our children were nine and eleven when my husband, claiming to be off for a two-week vacation, disappeared out West, leaving no forwarding address. At first I was relieved to be free of the constant tension and basked in the unexpected calm. But when the weeks stretched into months, with only an occasional call from a distant pay phone, and the children, as in my worst childhood fears, grew despondent and withdrawn, I became increasingly frantic. I had imagined a civilized divorce, with my husband ensconced somewhere across town, participating equally in child care, or at least seeing the children on alternate weekends. But he had something else in mind. Vacillating between remaining indefinitely in California with his lover and returning to us in New York, he made it clear that unless I took him back (or moved us all to California) the children might hardly ever see him.

Though I longed to be free of that husband, I was afraid to sacrifice our children, who were bewildered and betrayed by his disappearance and sinking daily before my eyes. I remember the exact moment I was stricken with a grim understanding of the stakes. The children, badly in need of cheering, had perked up visibly when I promised to take them one Sunday to the Bronx Zoo for the members' opening of an elaborate new birdhouse. Arranging our weekend outings had long been their father's province, but, determined to be mother and father at once, I packed us a picnic lunch, and off we set. My forced smiles turned hopeful when, emerging into the dazzling light from a gloomy hour-long subway ride, the children dashed up the stairs before me, carrying my sagging spirits with them. Which only made it harder when, fifteen minutes later, milling around the birdhouse entrance with a large crowd of animated families all waiting to get inside, I saw how lost and sad my children seemed. Suddenly I knew what it meant for a family to be broken. Broken, damaged, and—the word circled like a buzzard over their heads—*fatherless*, that most potent dread of my youth. Seeing my unhappy children watching the scores of happy ones sitting atop their fathers' shoulders or clasping each of their parents' hands, and remembering my own anguish as my baby brother was wrenched from my mother's arms, I feared it wouldn't be long before my childhood terrors smothered my adult desires.

If I'd known how resilient children of divorce can sometimes be or that divorced parents would be commonplace in the next generation, I might have held out. But I was a creature of my generation, not the next, and felt acutely my children's present suffering and looming catastrophe. I tried to be strong for them, but as the months went by, seeing them slide steadily into the pit of depression I slid down after them. Finally, the pain became unbearable, and less than a year after it started I gave up in defeat and summoned their father back.

When he returned, at first we were flooded with false expectations and blissful relief; our sex was never more passionate. But before long the rejoicing fizzled into resignation, and we reverted to what we were: a family of conflicts, crises, holidays, birthdays, and secrets. Without children we would certainly have divorced then, parting graciously and dividing our property neatly in half, as my first husband and I had done. Instead, until the children were grown, we arranged to spend as little time as possible together and still remain in a nominal marriage that was really divorce by other means.

WHAT I LEARNED

A decade later, when our arrangement finally disintegrated after twenty-five years of marriage (volatile years in which, fortunately, a lot more than mere marriage was going on in our lives), enough bitterness had collected that my second divorce was the customary nasty mess, the opposite of my first one. It dragged on for years instead of weeks, produced intransigence instead of compromise, exacted heartache and malice in place of regret, and cost half a fortune instead of the price of a trip to Mexico. By then our children, for whose sake we'd stayed tied, had gone off to college, but neither their age nor their absence protected them from the usual anguish and grief.

Now another decade has passed since our final papers were signed, and each of us has another mate. Still, my ex-husband can barely speak to me without an edge in his voice—which probably means our divorce is not yet final. How much longer will it take? A witty woman I know says that when lovers break up, getting over it takes about as long again as the pair were in love. But when children are involved, I wonder if the breakup of parents may not instead take about as long to get over as the age of the children when the breach occurred. Ours were four and six when my husband began wandering, nine and eleven when we first split up, nineteen and twenty-one when we filed for divorce. That means we may still have some time to go before all the acrimony has been dissipated and our accounts are fully settled (though, judging by how dispassionately I am able now to reflect on divorce, I suspect it is nearing closure). It may also mean—as our children have begun to suggest—that we could have divorced much sooner, that in the end it's unclear which is worse, a failed marriage or a failed divorce.

165

~~~

by

ALIX

KATES

SHULMAN

DIVORCE AS A SPECTATOR SPORT

BY *Francine Prose*

*S*OME TIME ago, a close friend arrived almost an hour late to a dinner party. She explained that while dressing to go out, she'd had the television on for company. And when an announcer promised an update on Roseanne and Tom Arnold's raucous ongoing marital breakup, my friend found herself sinking into her chair, quite unable to move until she'd heard what unscripted disruptive drama took place that day on the *Roseanne* set.

My friend is a poet and literary critic, known for her caustic wit, her low tolerance for banality, for sloppy thinking and sentimentality. But no one at the dinner table expressed the faintest surprise that this bright star of High Culture should have been pinned to her chair by a chance to metaphorically get down and mud wrestle with the Arnolds.

A brief silence fell on the dinner guests as we each tried to imagine what new and thrillingly tasteless celebrity psychodrama had caused our friend to come too late for the soup and nearly miss the main course. Then softly, almost reverentially, someone asked, "What happened with Tom and Roseanne?"

Divorce has always been a subject of passionate public and private interest. One can't help feeling that the cows in the fields and the seals on the rock turn their heads and take notice when the bull (or the bull seal) exchanges one mate for another. Curiosity about divorce is as old as divorce itself, which, as we know, the Old Testament and then the Koran made so blissfully easy (for men). The response to Henry VIII's divorce resulted in nothing less than the radical redesign of European history. When Dickens left the mother of his small army of children for a pretty young actress, readers on at least two continents reeled from the horror and shock, and though the divorces of Colette and Isak Dinesen may have generated less outrage, they were still the talk of Paris and colonial Kenya.

But for as long as the Church—and then Victorian social mores—had a tight repressive hold on popular culture and moral imagination, divorce was still mostly whispered about, tinged with secrecy and scandal. But now the stops are out, so to speak. Divorce is front-page news, and never has our hunger for the gritty facts been so insatiable and exquisite. In France, we hear, there is a new magazine called—what else?—*Divorce*. Demanding every intimate detail, we exhort our reporters and cameras to follow the warring couple, interrogate and eavesdrop, to bring us complete and unsparing reports from the bedrooms and the courtrooms.

Consider, for example, how Woody Allen's break with Mia Farrow generated more interest and discussion than most political campaigns. Everyone had an opinion, and debates became so heated that they often degenerated into personal attacks, into each sex accusing the other of the same bad attitudes and blind spots that are invariably recycled as live ammunition in each new flare-up of gender war.

As celebrity divorce grows increasingly more lurid and contentious, marital mishap has become a sort of spectator sport at which we can avidly follow the play-by-play. Centuries after the Romans abandoned their Colosseum, gruesome public divorce is what we have to take the place of bloodthirsty gladiatorial combat. And what's interesting to consider is what this curiosity means: What does our fascination with divorce say about us as a society, about our individual lives, our moral judgment, our marriages, our feminist sympathies, our hopes and fears, our integrity, our loyalties to ourselves, our spouses, our friends?

THERE'S ALMOST no point stating the obvious: that our society no longer respects or values personal privacy, that everything is seen as commerce, available information, every tiny fact accessible, the public's right to know. To want to keep one's own counsel and protect certain aspects of our lives from exposure is to risk being seen as neurotically withholding, or as being "in denial." Public figures who insist (often futilely) on their privacy are often described as "reclusive."

Meanwhile, confession is exalted not only as a therapeutic tool, an essential step toward recovery, but is assigned much the same value that used to be reserved for charity and good works. (One thinks of the celebrities wildly applauded and congratulated for bravely coming forward with accounts of personal crises that encourage fellow-sufferers to confront—and one hopes, solve—similar problems.)

And yet it seems to me that our voracious hunger to know about divorce far exceeds the parameters of what we've come to feel entitled to read in the newspaper or watch on tabloid TV. It's far more complex than the question of changing media attitudes, of the ways that the old rules have been reformulated by the gossip or self-help industries. It may well be that our desire to know about divorce—to watch it, as if it were indeed a spectator sport—is as innate as reflex or instinct, and as deep as our most profound feelings about love, sex, and death.

TO THINK ABOUT the meaning of our curiosity about divorce is to examine the nature of curiosity itself. The fact that we want so badly to know, and that certain privileged information seems so titillating and delicious, is a sign of how profoundly it touches on our deepest hopes and fears. Trivial subjects are never taboo. But the great mysteries often are—in particular, the endlessly fascinating and (despite the new climate of "openness") still mysterious subjects of sex and death.

Partly what intrigues us about divorce is its intimations of secrets concerning sex and death, or at least the death of love. Divorce represents the dark side of the mating instinct—an instinct about which we will never lose our inquisitiveness and interest. Even in highly civilized, amicable separations, we intuit that the fact of divorce hints at some serious discord, misunderstanding or cruelty, sexual boredom or fatigue. It may be that couples do split up over the question of who does the laundry and dishes, but the helping professions are quick to remind us that something more important is usually at stake.

Perhaps that's the reason why nothing whets our appetite quite so much as the dissolution of those marriages that had seemed, on the surface, perfect. The unpleasant secrets, we feel, were more hidden, more closely guarded, buried deeper and therefore more valuable and more satisfying to exhume.

What we most yearn to know about divorce is who did what to whom (or stopped doing what to whom), who fell in love with someone else, who got violent, abused this or that substance, or in some way proved so difficult or impossible to live with that whatever passion or affinity had drawn the couple together began to seem like a big mistake, a costly *folie à deux.*

Years ago, the reasons (or the stated reasons) for divorce were relatively simple and straightforward: A man had tired of his wife and perhaps found someone new— or learned that his wife had dared to look at, possibly even found, someone new. But now that women have the legal and social option of initiating divorce, the possible reasons for ending a marriage have multiplied and our speculative interest has also grown to match the endless variant imaginary scenarios that divorce brings to mind.

Our hunger to know the facts of divorce is connected to our drive to understand love—and the opposite sex. Often, as I hear my friends talking about the breakup of people we know or of stars we've never met, I'm reminded of how, as young girls, we got together and jabbered fervidly in search of some clue to the puzzle of why people fall in love—and, by implication, the riddle of how to make boys fall in love with us.

What we're asking when we ask about divorce is how people fall out of love. And if, as girls, we searched for answers about what boys really wanted, what we're asking, as adults, is what men and women *don't* want—what causes them to take a stand, to draw the line, to divorce.

The questions we pose, the information we seek from accounts of private or public divorce, are strikingly like the things we ask about death, the ways in which we read obituaries. How and why did it happen? What was it like? Was it accidental or inevitable? Who, if anyone, was at fault?

And what we're really asking is not strictly about the deceased or the divorcing couple. If we're honest, we're obliged to admit that our real (or at least partial) subject is ourselves. We may be seeking reassurance that the dead and the divorced were not like us—that they did reckless things that we would never do, smoked or drank, forgot to exercise, had unsafe sex, cheated on their spouses—so that the tragic thing that happened to them cannot possibly happen to us.

Alternately, we may realize that they are very much like us, and that what has befallen them is certainly (in the case of death) or possibly (with divorce) in our own futures (or already in our pasts). In which case, what we're asking is: What exactly was it like? How protracted was it? How painful? Was it like *my* divorce, like what happened to me? How did they get through it, and recover—or not?

Obviously, the questions we ask and the way in which we ask them have much to do with our own domestic situations (whether we're married, divorced, or single), with the health of our romantic relationships, and with our basic feelings about the institution of marriage. I've noticed, for example, that a number of my gay male friends are often more enthralled, disappointed, and horrified than I am by the details of divorce; quite a few seem to hold a sweetly romanticized vision of heterosexual marriage, a view mostly unavailable to straight men and women who have, through bitter experience, exchanged that idyllic notion for a healthy cynicism which allows them to be continually surprised (as I am) when a marriage works out.

Those who have already been divorced may find in the news of high- or low-profile divorce a reassuring sense of solidarity and camaraderie. Especially for the newly divorced, whose memories are still fresh and often wounding, each new public breakup may serve as a mirror for their own experience, a glass in which they can see yet another couple joining the legions of those who have been through it. Meanwhile the much-divorced and the determinedly single may see each divorce as confirmation of the statistically demonstrable fact that marriage is a lousy idea, hopelessly doomed from the start, with a history of disaster going all the way back to the Garden of Eden. Men and women, such cynics say, were not created, biologically or psychologically, to live together for very long in anything remotely resembling monogamous harmony.

I CAN REMEMBER intervals in my life when I found myself living with a man whom I had ceased to love and no longer wanted to live with, but whom—because of my own laziness, inertia, and lack of sufficiently powerful motivation—I was unable to leave. In some cases, it took me a very long time to realize or admit to myself that I wanted to be on my own.

Perhaps what should have tipped me off was the puzzling fact that whenever I heard that friends (or even celebrities) were splitting up, I was suffused with vague inchoate yearning and with something like the jealousy I imagine prisoners experience on learning that one of their jailmates has made a successful escape. I followed accounts of divorce almost as if I were trying to comprehend a set of how-to instructions: Who announced he or she was leaving? What exactly was said? How much commotion ensued? How long did it take before they were—separately—happy again?

Conversely, there were times when, in the throes of an unhappy love affair or just after a romance had ended, I was drawn to stories of divorce much as the newly diagnosed collect optimistic anecdotes about intrepid long-term survivors of life-threatening illnesses. At such times, many of the greatest heroines of literature and history (again, Isak Dinesen and Colette) were reduced in my own damaged mind and heart to exemplars of women who had endured rocky marriages, painful divorces—and not only survived, but prevailed.

As I write this, at this point in my life, my situation seems quite different. My husband and I have been together happily (knock on wood) for almost twenty years. And though I know that there are many divorced men and women who once beguiled themselves with the same naive fantasies, my bet is that it will be death (and not divorce) that will finally divide us.

Now when I hear accounts of divorce, I feel much the same sinking dread with which I react to news of untimely illness and death. I've become one of those who watch spectator divorce for reassurance that my husband and I are not at all like that warring couple: that there's not a chance we're making Roseanne and Tom Arnold's mistakes.

Not long ago, we visited with a friend in the midst of a divorce as seemingly lacking in rancor as divorce can conceivably be. Normally a sympathetic, soft-spoken man whom friends call in tears when their old dogs must be put to sleep or when their pipes have frozen and burst in the dead of winter, my husband began asking our friend a series of questions so personal and pointed, so oddly harsh and so intent on assigning guilt and blame that the tension in the room mounted dismayingly until at last our friend laughed and wisely said, "Come on, would you relax? It's not going to happen to you!" And I have to admit that it pleased me to hear that my husband was so threatened and upset by the idea that a couple—not unlike ourselves— could have decided to call it quits.

What makes it all the more complicated—especially when it's friends who are divorcing—is when our response to the separation moves beyond the realm of personal prayer (Please don't let this happen to us) and into the realm of moral or quasi-moral judgment. In such cases we're quick (often too quick) to decide who the guilty party is and who has been grievously wronged. We recreate, in ourselves, miniature Family Courts and get to play judge and juror.

This is often what makes celebrity divorce so much like an athletic event, a football game, a tennis match, or prizefight. We choose our favorite players and cheer them on, often quite rabidly, championing their cause against those fools who are deluded or stupid enough to root for the opposite side.

Once again, personal projection comes into play and may interfere with the higher principles of strict jurisprudence. Consequently, it comes as less than a shock that our sympathies in these cases so often seem gender-determined.

Surely there are many men who secretly suspected that those who failed to see, say, Woody Allen's point of view were mostly women whose instinctively clear understanding of passion, love, and sex had been permanently clouded by a murky fog of life-denying feminism. But the truth is that many women know from harsh experience (or at least from a friend's harsh experience) what it's like to see a man wake up one day and suddenly realize that he himself will magically cease to age if he sleeps with a younger woman.

When a couple breaks up, the men in their circle of friends may express considerable shock that the wife could have given up such a wonderful, thoughtful guy, while the women may be equally amazed that the wife could have patiently endured the bragging egomaniacal bully for as long as she did. And certainly the media are not unaware of this tendency to choose sides. Editors and producers know that the gender conflict simmering away beneath the deceptively placid surface of our daily lives will boil over reliably in response to well-publicized divorces; the sex war is what gives such stories their heat, their currency, and the staying power that keeps them on our front pages and TV screens long after the quarrelsome couple itself grows bored with its own complaints and accusations.

Again, it's more complicated when the divorcing couple are friends — that is, when we've long believed that both members of the couple are friends we value and cherish equally. It's well known that despite our most heartfelt resolve, we are frequently forced to choose sides. In such cases, our harmless little game of domestic court judge-and-jury takes on graver consequences: a friendship or, in many instances, two friendships are at stake.

What's disturbing is how frequently our sense of morality, justice, and fair play is subordinated to other, more shallow (or perhaps just more visceral) concerns. Though we may know beyond any doubt that the husband or wife was the innocent — or the guilty — party, we still may be chagrined to discover that we are drawn to stay friends with the one who amuses us more, the one whom we find more interesting: the one we simply like better, regardless of his or her sins against the aggrieved spouse.

It's happened to me more often than I'd choose to admit, and it's always painful — but in a way, a welcome reminder that I'm less high-minded and fair than I might wish to imagine. But isn't this also a part of what it means to be human? We're complicated, unruly, and susceptible when our hearts overrule our brains, when our instincts win out against what we call our "better instincts."

Perhaps that's something to consider when we sink into our chairs and watch Tom Arnold inform the cameras how much he still loves Roseanne, or Woody Allen tell a barrage of flashbulbs that he never molested his children. It's theater, it's show biz: Mad Max on the information superhighway. It's gladiatorial combat — but real blood's being spilled, even if Roseanne and Tom are inventing the whole thing for publicity and will reconcile in time for tomorrow's *Entertainment Tonight*.

Someone is almost always in pain just beneath the endlessly fascinating surface of public divorce. And yet for many reasons, some good, some bad—but all equally basic to our human nature and therefore comprehensible— we can't stop ourselves from watching the combatants flail away, each of us a Roman emperor or empress, smiling or frowning, applauding or hissing, turning our thumbs up or down.

IN THE

COUNTRY OF DIVORCE

Confessions of a Soon-To-Be-Divorcée

BY *Daphne Merkin*

1. THE LAY OF THE LAND

Who could know it would be this way—that you enter the country of divorce at your own peril and leave it a changed person? (If and when you leave: Be prepared to stay awhile; bring plenty of clean underwear and reading matter; but most of all, bring lots of cash.) Who could know, given the fact that divorce rolls so trippingly off the tip of the cultural tongue these days—everyone's doing it, at least one out of two couples—that you'd think it would be easy, or at least not all that hard.

Well, think again. The breakup of a marriage, American-style—especially if there's a child involved—is more in the spirit of war than you'd believe possible of a negotiation involving two people who once slept side by side. Amiable instances are rumored to exist, although I have personally yet to encounter one. It's a rough sport, this divorcing game, and the financial bloodletting is not the worst of it. I realize that each person's experience is unique, but what I've discovered these past three long—*very* long—years is that a process that began in dire seriousness gradually took on, somewhere into the second year when my exhusband-to-be and I sat for hours in a shabby courtroom with peeling walls while our lawyers chatted and the judge listened to other cases, an atmosphere of the surreal. What was I doing here, in a near-empty room dominated by an American flag and a feeling of grim supplication? (Most divorces don't get as far as a courtroom, but once they do you're placing your fate in the hands of what you better hope will be justice.) And how would I ever get out?

In our beginnings are our ends, only in some of our cases the beginnings never get off the ground. I got married in a sea of doubts, a thicket of anxieties—pick whichever metaphor of turmoil you prefer, and it would apply—and although I suppose for some reluctant brides the institution of matrimony in itself exerts a certain calming influence, in my case I remained a reluctant bride from first to last. I say none of this happily, but it seems to me that it's important to tell the truth about one's own circumstances if one is to shed any light at all. My marriage had its besetting problems, yet I've come to think that what distinguishes a marriage which lasts from one that doesn't isn't how good or bad the union in question is but how tolerable the partners find it to be. We all know of atrocious marriages that continue to drip, Jackson Pollock–like, across the canvas of life until the death of one of the spouses, and of wobbly but not inherently hopeless ones that topple over before you can say Raoul Felder.

What I'm trying to suggest is that there's some sort of psychic bartering that goes on within most enduring marriages—he's a bore at dinner parties, but he pays for the clothes and the shrink, or she's a bitch most of the time and still hasn't learned how to cook, but she looks great on his arm—that doesn't get articulated in public, because it's not in anyone's interest to do so. The great Marxist theoreticians notwithstanding, most cultures are profoundly conservative in nature. And marriage, how-ever it gets reconfigured from time to time, is indubitably part of the proven way of doing things: It works, more or less; besides which, no one's figured out a better way of ensuring that the male of the human species sits down to breakfast with the female on an ongoing basis.

This, at any rate, is how I've come to see it, over in the muddy marshes of Divorce Country where I've gotten bogged down: Marriage is a complex, partial satisfaction of myriad needs—sexual, romantic, and economic. The institution varies so radically from one couple to the next as to lack all criterion of the "normative." There are those spouses who function with an almost claustrophobic qual-ity of togetherness; others who prefer to live in different cities. But somewhere along the way, no matter what a particular marriage looks like from the outside in, the two people involved have to feel comfortable with how their respective sides of the equation tally. Contrary to advice-column wisdom, which has it that the small conflicts are what eventually do a marriage in, it is my belief that the big conflicts—clashing notions of intimacy, say, rather than tension over putting caps on toothpaste tubes—are what land two people in real trouble. I, for instance, married a man who left me feeling lonely not because he wasn't home but because he *was*. I found myself circling him nervously, my troth plighted to this alien presence plopped down in the middle of first my one-bedroom and then our three-bedroom apartment, until the day came when I stuffed two suitcases full of courage and ran for the hills. I felt like one of the von Trapp family at the end of *The Sound of Music*, scrambling over the mountains that linked neutral Switzerland to Nazi Austria; I didn't know if I'd survive the journey, but I knew staying where I was would doom me to a worse fate than the one which lay ahead.

2. CROSSING THE BORDER

I am lying in bed at two, three in the morning. My one-and-a-half-year-old daughter is asleep in her crib in her room with its lovingly chosen toys and stenciled border of pastel-colored ducklings. I have watched TV, read a sprinkling of magazines, and still I cannot fall asleep due to the anxiety that clutches at my chest. I begin making lists in my head, dividing categories into subcategories— an activity that has often soothed me in the past: How many divorced women do I know? Divorced women with children? Divorced women without children? Divorced women who have remarried? Failed to remarry? How long do you have to have been married before you get divorced for it to look like you've given it the old college try and aren't a complete failure? (If I stretch things, and include the months my husband refused to move out of the apartment and slept on a chaise longue in the living room, it just makes the three-year mark. Which means I've been getting divorced as long as I've been married.) I look up at the ceiling and start enumerating my virtues as a marital partner for the benefit of the Great Judge in the sky: long legs, good hair, intelligence, wit, empathy, and erratic kindness. He shakes his head at me, and in my heart of hearts I know he recognizes that I am an inadequate person. Why else would I be getting a divorce?

3. TRAVEL TIPS
FOR FIRST-TIME VISITORS

Divorce is a country that doesn't recognize the high road; once you enter it, be prepared to put aside any mainland principles about decency and fairness. I'm on my second lawyer—third, if you count the lawyer I went to for several meetings before I decided she would prove too expensive. The next lawyer I saw was a partner in a less prominent firm; he was a softhearted, perennially distracted sort who I think I chose because he made me feel less guilty about standing up for myself. (My guilt had much to do with the fact that it was I who initiated divorce proceedings; the fact that my husband immediately retaliated by suing for sole custody of our daughter should have gone a long way toward assuaging that guilt, but strangely did not.) I had been told that this lawyer was "good for women"—and he did, indeed, seem to harbor little animus against either sex. But he also seemed to expend minimal energy on my behalf, and as the months went by and my phone calls went unreturned and my husband continued to live in our apartment *even though I had already filed for divorce,* loudly finding fault with my every move as a mother (his specialty was to emit a mirthless chuckle whenever I spoke up against his rigid ideas about child rearing, as if to suggest that I was the last person to have any say in these matters), I realized I would have to make a change.

The lawyer I have retained since then is a smart, scrappy woman in practice for herself. My relationship with her has been tempestuous; it has survived any number of confrontations, ranging from her criticism regarding the tone of the message on my answering machine ("too flaky") to my criticism regarding her style of giving me instructions ("authoritarian"). My lawyer is involved in the feminist end of law, which initially alarmed as much as it attracted me: I wanted to make sure she understood that I was not getting my divorce on behalf of the women's movement and was not interested in taking a rhetorical—if right-minded—position that would endanger my chances.

Truth be told, there is nothing like a divorce to make a Madonna out of a Tammy Wynette. Nothing like a divorce, that is, to make even the most accommodating and least politicized female sit up and take note of the fact that the judicial system is run primarily by men who tend on the whole to favor women who stay home and busy themselves with *kinder* and *küche*—and to regard with punitive suspicion (however unconscious) those women who want it every which way, the career and the children and the divorce. In this regard, the more vociferous and unyielding claims of the women's movement (which include the devaluation of motherhood and the insistence on a theoretical egalitarianism at home) have done an inadvertent disservice to divorcing professional women who also happen to be passionate mothers. It's a strange phenomenon, hard to understand until you're caught in the middle of it, but all the tradition-bound attitudes that men were left to struggle with in the last three decades while women were busy taking great strides forward to a new tomorrow seem to coalesce over the issue of child custody. "In the fifties," observes a psychiatrist I know, "you could shoot up heroin and you'd still get the child because you were the mother." These days fathers who want to be the custodial parent tend to be given the benefit of the doubt (up to 40 percent petition for custody, the majority of whom win), and the burden of proof has been shifted onto mothers, especially if they work outside the home.

4. LEARNING THE LANGUAGE

A question: Why is the vocabulary of divorce so woefully underdeveloped? I can understand how long ago in the dark ages of divorce, when unmarried women were still referred to as spinsters and the dubious concept of "quality time" hadn't yet been developed, the need for a more fluid terminology was scant: Divorce, when and if it happened, took place expeditiously, with the children generally assumed to remain with the mother. But now that divorce has become a thing of custody suits which stretch on for years, of forensic psychiatrists who painstakingly conduct interviews and pay house visits as though one or other of the parties dabbled in serial murder, of legal counsel that gets paid astronomic fees by the hour

and remains in one's employ longer than most housekeep-
ers, I surely can't be the first person to find herself at a
descriptive loss. Who is my daughter's father to me now
that we are no longer married but not yet divorced? I'm
talking semantics, never mind the more existential stuff:
Is he, linguistically speaking, my *ex-husband-to-be,* which
sounds like a mangled form of the future perfect, or
should I refer to him as my *estranged husband,* which
sounds even clumsier, as though he's been swallowed by a
whale?

5. GOING NATIVE

Sex seems so far away, an island that's floated farther
and farther off since I've been living alone. In the beginning of my divorce I didn't think about sex much, lost as
I was in feelings that precluded erotic pleasure, feelings
that had to do with ancient conflicts about the "wrong-
ness" or "rightness" of my very being. Perhaps I wasn't
lovable (even though it was I who wanted out); perhaps I
didn't know how to love. How to explain this abiding
sense of shame, this lingering feeling that it was all my own
fault? I might remark that I find it curious that over the
last three years not one person among my wide circle of
friends has asked me how it feels to live alone—physically
alone—after living with a man. It is as if my sexual feelings
have become taboo, a link to the banished privileges of
the connubial bed. . . .

These days, I find myself going into bookstores and
furtively looking at the section that carries titles on divorce and child custody, hoping not to be spotted. After I

buy the books they lie, unread, on my night table as I escape into the romantic world of late-night movies; it seems I am not willing to become part of the divorced population on so official a level. When I'm not avoiding the subject altogether, I keep trying to figure out the reasons for my unease. True, there is the fact that I come from an Orthodox Jewish background where divorce is relatively infrequent, and all five of my siblings are married to their original spouses. But I gave up being Orthodox years ago and I now move in a world where divorce is rife. So how to explain it?

Ah, here we come upon the gap—crevasse, actually—between the statistical reality which is bruited about in magazines and the reality which is felt by one nonstatistical adult female within the context of her daily life. To wit: Divorce may not have the stigma it once had, but it is still cause for anxiety. Marriage, as one of my restlessly married friends says, is a "cover," a form of social armor: You can go to parties and announce "this is my husband" and the world will smile upon you as one of their suitably partnered own. The divorced woman suggests, by her very presence, a threat to the status quo; she carries with her the subliminal risk of her own instability, her lack of conviction about so important a decision as who she should marry. Worse yet, there is the dark aura of her singleness, and the accompanying specter of emotional neediness. Worst of all, she intimates at the possibility that the marriages around her are themselves as likely to fall apart as not. Present yourself as a married woman and you are free to indulge in "safe flirting"; present yourself as a divorced woman and you are perceived as a potentially dangerous predator.

It is the end of May, a weekend afternoon on the cusp of summer, breezy and shining, not yet oppressively hot. I am sitting on the benches facing Manhattan's East River, with a Walkman and a book. On the promenade behind me people amble, run, ride bikes, and parade by in a joyous celebration of family life—arms entwined, offspring perched on shoulders or gurgling in strollers. Everyone's a pair, everyone's been married for years, even the young-looking couples have an air of longstanding domestic contentment. Or so it seems to me, sitting by myself even though I am the mother of a four-and-a-half-year-old daughter, even though ten months before my daughter was born I got married in my parents' living room to a man I had known for six years. I am a woman in the middle of a divorce that seems to have gone on forever, and today my daughter is with her father, leaving me to my own devices.

I lean down to pick up a page of a local, residential newspaper that has landed near my bench. An advertisement in bold type catches my eye: It turns out to be for a group that meets weekly to discuss the anxieties and difficulties of people going through divorce. This could be taken for a sign from above, except that I am uncomfortable with the notion of divorce, painful as it is, being converted into yet another arm of the endlessly proliferating support-group industry. Then, too, I find it impossible to imagine discussing my concerns with complete strangers: Is there an amorous future after divorce? Will there ever be a second husband? How am I to define myself now that I'm no longer that solemn creature known as A Wife—

now that I've blown off the man I vowed to honor, cherish, and respect until death did us part? I recognize, of course, that I have other parts left to play—as writer, friend, mother, daughter, sister, aunt—but they all seem to pale next to this lapsed one: Once I was married, the wife of X; now I am not.

7. DREAMING OF ELSEWHERE

Not long ago I bought a video called "Divorce Can Happen to the Nicest People," since to this day I find it unbearably sad to discuss with my daughter why her parents no longer live together. Oh, I've trotted out all the *Good Housekeeping* seal-of-approval phrases and explained that no, I didn't think we'd all be one family again, and yes, Daddy and I both loved her the same as we always had even though we couldn't get along with each other. But there is something in me that rebels against the whole tinny enterprise of justifying inchoate adult behavior to a little girl grappling with abstract concepts like love and constancy and sorrow. So on a recent Saturday night the two of us cuddled up in my bed to watch the video. There was nothing precisely wrong with the film except that it failed to hold our attention. The most interesting thing about it for me was that the screenplay was by Peter Mayle—who went on to write the phenomenally successful books about going to live in Provence with his family. The video wasn't half over before Zoë had fallen asleep next to me, her mouth slightly open, her arms askew. I leaned over to give her a kiss, and then I lay in the dark, wondering whether Peter Mayle had written about divorce from personal experience, whether my own life might change dramatically for the better after my divorce became final, and whether I would create a new family with the man I loved and go on to write best-sellers . . . and the horrendous particulars of my first marriage—the bickering and taunting and twisting of intimate details into weapons—would fade away. . . .

8. LETTER FROM ABROAD

When I think about my divorce I keep coming back to the opening sentence of L. P. Hartley's *The Go-Between,* one of those gently cadenced British novels that is eerily familiar with the bleaker aspects of human behavior: "The past is a foreign country: They do things differently there." If you paraphrase the quote, it could apply just as well to the permanent present tense in which the breakup of marriages takes place: *Divorce is a foreign country: They do things differently there.* If I've learned anything from my sojourn in this strange land, it's that I'm made of tougher stuff than I once thought I was. You're born alone, you die alone, and you get divorced alone. It's taken me a while to wrap my mind around that obdurate fact, but now that I've finally adjusted to the chilly landscape I'm looking forward to making my way back one of these days to friendlier climes. Beyond the horizon of divorce shimmers the vista of Life-after-Divorce. I'm sure it's a terrain filled with potholes and roadblocks all its own, but from where I'm standing it looks like nothing less than paradise.

ABOUT
THE CONTRIBUTORS

DIANA HUME GEORGE is a professor of English at Penn State at Erie, The Behrend College. She is also a poet, essayist, and critic whose books include *Blake and Freud, Oedipus Anne: The Poetry of Anne Sexton,* and *The Resurrection of the Body.* She edited *Sexton: Selected Criticism,* and, with Diane Wood Middlebrook, *The Selected Poems of Anne Sexton.* Her poetry, essays, interviews, and reviews have appeared in numerous periodicals, and in the *Best American Essays.* Her book of feminist travel essays, *The Lonely Other: A Woman Watching America,* is forthcoming.

ELLEN GILCHRIST is author of twelve books of fiction, poetry, and essays. Her latest book is *The Age of Miracles.*

ANN HOOD is the author of six novels, including *The Properties of Water, Places to Stay the Night,* and *Somewhere Off the Coast of Maine.* Her essays, reviews, and short stories have appeared in many magazines and newspapers, including the *New York Times,* the *Washington Post, Redbook, Glamour, Seventeen, Self,* and *Story.* She is a contributing editor at *Parenting* magazine and lives in Providence, Rhode Island.

PENNY KAGANOFF is a senior editor at Simon & Schuster. Formerly, she was editor-in-chief of *Kirkus Reviews,* a book review editor at *Publishers Weekly,* a columnist for the *New York Daily News,* and a judge for the National Book Critics Circle Awards. Her essays and criticism have appeared in a number of newspapers and magazines. She lives in Brooklyn, New York.

PERRI KLASS is the author of two novels, *Other Women's Children* and *Recombinations,* a collection of short stories, *I Am Having an Adventure,* and two volumes of nonfiction, *A Not Entirely Benign Procedure: Four Years as a Medical Student* and *Baby Doctor: A Pediatrician's Training.* Her short fiction has received five O. Henry Awards. She is a pediatrician in Boston, and is on the faculty of the Boston University School of Medicine.

DAPHNE MERKIN is the author of a novel, *Enchantment.* She is a judge for the National Book Critics Circle Awards and is on the editorial board of *Partisan Review.* She has contributed essays to the *New Yorker,* the

New York Times, Esquire, Mirabella, and other periodicals. Her second novel, *The Discovery of Sex,* and a collection of essays, *Fear and Trembling & Life Notes,* are forthcoming from Simon & Schuster. She lives in New York City with her daughter, Zoë.

MARY MORRIS is the author of two collections of short stories, two travel memoirs, and three novels, the most recent of which is *A Mother's Love.* She has also co-edited the travel anthology, *Maiden Voyages.* Her numerous short stories and travel essays have appeared in the *Paris Review,* the *New York Times,* and *Vogue.* The recipient of a Guggenheim Fellowship and the Rome Prize in Literature, she teaches writing at Sarah Lawrence College and lives in Brooklyn.

ANN PATCHETT is the author of two novels, *The Patron Saint of Liars* and *Taft.* She graduated from Sarah Lawrence College and the Iowa Writer's Workshop, served as a fellow at the Mary Ingraham Bunting Institute at Radcliffe College, and is the recipient of a Guggenheim Fellowship. Currently, she lives in Nashville, Tennessee.

FRANCINE PROSE is the author of nine novels, including *Bigfoot Dreams, Primitive People,* and *Hunters and Gatherers,* as well as two story collections: *Women and Children First* and *The Peaceable Kingdom.* Her stories and essays have appeared in *Best American Stories,* the *New Yorker, The Atlantic, Condé Nast Traveler, Antaeus, The Yale Review,* and the *New York Times Book Review.* She lives in upstate New York.

ANNE ROIPHE is the author of the novels *Up the Sandbox, Torch Song, Lovingkindness,* and *If You Knew Me,* and the nonfiction books *Generation without Memory* and *A Season for Healing: Reflections on the Holocaust.* She is a columnist for the *New York Observer* and a contributor to the *Jerusalem Report.*

JANE SHAPIRO's first novel, *After Moondog,* was a finalist for a *Los Angeles Times* Book Prize. Her story, "Poltergeists," which originally appeared in the *New Yorker,* is included in *The Best American Short Stories 1993.* Her short fiction and journalism have been published in the *New Yorker,* the *New York Times,* the *Village Voice, Mirabella,* and many others. She has taught fiction writing at Rutgers University and lives in Princeton.

CAROL SHIELDS has written two books of short stories and seven novels, most recently *The Stone Diaries,* which won the Pulitzer Prize, the National Book Critics Circle Award, and the Canadian Governor-General's Award. She grew up in Oak Park, Illinois, and now lives in Winnipeg, Canada, where she teaches at the University of Manitoba.

ALIX KATES SHULMAN is a political activist, feminist, teacher, and writer whose novels include *Memoirs of an Ex-Prom Queen, Burning Questions, On the Stroll,* and *In Every Woman's Life.* . . . Her essays have appeared in the *Nation, Atlantic Monthly,* and the *New York Times Book Review.* Her newest book is the memoir, *Drinking the Rain.* Ms. Shulman has taught at the University of Hawaii, Yale, and New York University, has been a visiting artist at the American Academy in Rome, and has received NEA and DeWitt Wallace/Reader's Digest fellowships. She divides her time between New York City and an island off the coast of Maine.

SUSAN SPANO is a graduate of Mount Holyoke College and a former fiction editor for *Redbook*. Her articles have appeared in the *New York Times Book Review, New York Newsday,* and *New Woman.* As the author of The Frugal Traveler column in the *New York Times Travel Section,* she travels widely and frequently. Her home is Manhattan's West Village.